A Taste of the Valley

The People, The Vineyards, The Wineries,
And The Recipes of The Alexander Valley

The Alexander Valley Winegrowers
Sonoma County, California

This book has many authors. The editors of the Hoffman Press wish to express their appreciation to them for their assembly of these histories and recipes of the Alexander Valley. These authors are the people of the wineries and vineyards of the Valley who took the time and made the effort to tell the stories of their vineyards and wineries and to give us their very best recipes. We are indebted, too, to the professional chefs, who created some of the recipes in this book. Special thanks go to Susan Rice, the manager of the Alexander Valley Winegrowers.

We also wish to note the contributions of John Nelson, our photographer, who spent weeks in the field shooting many photos for our selection. We were truly fortunate to find him. A native of Sonoma County, he has an intimate knowledge of the wine industry. He is a Sonoma County champion grape stomper! His photographs have won many blue ribbons and awards.

The photographs of the cover and four seasons of the vineyard year are by George Rose of Allied Domecq, and we are indebted to him for his generosity in allowing their usage here.

Alexander Valley Winegrowers
P.O. Box 248
Healdsburg, California 95448

For information on the Wines and Wineries of Alexander Valley and to order your copy of **A Taste of the Valley,** please visit www.alexandervalley.org or call 1-888-289-4637.

Printed in Korea

A Taste of the Valley

A Map of the Valley

The Wineries

1. Alexander Valley Vineyards
2. Canyon Road Winery
3. Chateau Souverain
4. Clos du Bois Wines
5. de Lorimier Winery
6. Field Stone Winery
7. Geyser Peak Winery
8. Hanna Winery
9. Hart's Desire Wines
10. Johnson's Alexander Valley Wines
11. Jordan Vineyard & Winery
12. Kendall-Jackson Wine Country Store
13. Murphy-Goode Estate Winery
14. Sausal Winery
15. Seghesio Family Vineyards
16. Silver Oak Cellars
17. Simi Winery
18. Stonestreet Winery
19. Trentadue Winery
20. White Oak Winery
21. Wattle Creek

61 Miles To Mendocino

194 Miles To Eureka

Cloverdale

Russian River

ALEXANDER VALLEY

Geyserville Ave

Chianti Rd.

Dutcher Creek

Geyserville

CANYON RD EXIT

Canyon Rd.

Dry Creek Rd

INDEPENDENCE LANE EXIT

Lytton Springs Rd.

Alexander Valley Rd

Russian River

16 Miles To Calistoga

Healdsburg

Thomas Rd.

Chalk Hill Rd.

70 Miles To San Francisco

5

Introduction

A HERITAGE OF VINES AND WINES

Alexander Valley has a history of vines and wine as big—and as varied—as the landscape from which it originates. Today's vintners and growers add to a wine heritage nearly 150 years in the making, with the same pioneer spirit that has characterized Alexander Valley from the beginning.

Cyrus Alexander, for whom Alexander Valley is named, planted the region's first vineyard in 1846. A former mountain man, Alexander came to the valley in 1841 to manage the Sotoyome Rancho for Captain Henry Fitch. As payment for his services, he received 9,000 acres on the eastern side of the valley four years later. There he built a home and planted a vineyard and orchard, using trees and vines originally obtained from the abandoned Russian outpost at Fort Ross, 45 miles away. History does not record whether Alexander made wine from his grapes, but circumstantial evidence suggests he did.

In the three decades following the Gold Rush of 1849, the population of Alexander Valley grew slowly. While wheat was the region's dominant crop, orchards and vineyards were increasingly common. H. Kier established the valley's first winery in Cloverdale in 1872; four years later Giuseppe and Peitro Simi built a stone winery north of Healdsburg. By 1875, an estimated 230 acres in Alexander Valley were devoted to vineyards.

The 1880s and early 1890s were a period of explosive growth for both vineyards and wineries in Alexander Valley. By 1885, vineyard acreage in the valley had jumped to an estimated 1,500 acres, half of which was planted to Zinfandel. Ten new wineries opened during this era, including Geyser Peak Winery in 1880, Italian Swiss Colony in 1887, and the Chase Winery (owned by Horace Chase, founder of Napa Valley's Stag's Leap Winery) in 1893. For a time, Geyserville was home to both the largest brandy making facility in the United States and a major must condensing factory, which produced grape concentrate for home winemakers. Alexander Valley grapes were considered among the best in California, fetching premium prices from wineries in other regions.

The boom was over by 1900, as falling wine prices and the ravages of Phylloxera took their toll in Alexander Valley. Some vineyards were replanted on resistant rootstock; others were removed to make way for prunes, apples, pears, and hops. A few wineries opened after 1900, but many more closed. Following the enactment of Prohibition in 1920, only two Alexander Valley wineries remained in business (by producing sacramental wine and concentrate), but growers who had replanted their vineyards found a ready market for their grapes among home winemakers.

The repeal of Prohibition in 1933 did little to improve Alexander Valley's wine fortunes, though some wineries closed by Prohibition reopened, and a scattering of new wineries was established. Economic depression, World War II and frequent oversupply made earning a living from wine a difficult proposition. By 1964, the valley was home to just eight wineries.

Alexander Valley's renaissance as wine country began quietly in 1956 with a single vineyard, the first new vineyard to be planted in the region in nearly two decades. Vineyard development accelerated in the 1960s and 1970s, with new grape varieties and modern viticultural techniques restoring Alexander Valley's reputation for exceptional grapes. The resurgence in vineyards was followed by a resurgence in winemaking, as old wineries were revitalized and new wineries were built. In 1973, new and longtime residents joined forces in support of zoning to preserve Alexander Valley's agricultural identity.

In recent years, the region's wine industry has continued to grow and prosper. Alexander Valley's 11,000 acres of vineyards now supply more than 25 local wineries—and perhaps twice as many in other regions—with varietal grapes of unmatched quality. Establishment of Alexander Valley as an American Viticultural Area in 1984 has enabled wineries using Alexander Valley grapes to feature the appellation on their labels. Finally, Cabernet Sauvignon, Merlot, Zinfandel, Chardonnay, Sauvignon Blanc and Gewürztraminer from Alexander Valley have each earned reputations for distinctive regional character.

An Alexander Valley Pioneer

Rose Demostene Benson

Rose Demostene is a lifelong resident of Alexander Valley and Healdsburg. She is the daughter of Abele Ferrari, who founded the Healdsburg Machine Shop and was part-owner of the historic Soda Rock Winery; wife of the late Leo Demostene, rancher and grape grower; and mother of the four Demostene siblings who founded and manage the well-known Sausal Winery.

Rose's father, Abele, came from Savigliano, Italy in the early 1900s to establish the Healdsburg Machine Shop. He and his partners built the Healdsburg Grape Crusher for the many small wineries stretching from Calistoga to Cloverdale. This crusher is still used at many wineries today.

Rose, his oldest daughter, grew up in Healdsburg attending local schools and obtaining a degree in education from the University of California, Berkeley. She remembers when there were quicksilver mines in the hills above the valley at what is now known as Pine Flat, and when her father helped harness the first steam wells up at the geysers. The ride up the mountain was in a Model A, and the whole family would have to get out and push the car across the creeks. Her mother always brought eggs that they could hard boil in the "Devil's Cauldron."

After she completed her higher education, she returned to Healdsburg, married Leo Demostene, and, together with her parents, bought the Soda Rock Winery in Alexander Valley. The Soda Rock Ranch harvested six crops—apples, pears, prunes, grapes and walnuts. Rose did the book work, paid the bills, sold grapes and bulk wine, and even worked in the fields overseeing the harvest.

She remembers one year with dread as she watched the rain for a solid week while the grapes sat in boxes waiting to be picked up and taken to the crusher. It was the fall of 1943 and they still used horses to pull sleds down the rows to pile the full boxes on. By the time the horses could get through the field, the grapes were only fit as distilling material.

In the early years, varieties such as Alicante Bouchet, Golden Chassels, Palomino and Grenache were commonplace in the valley and on the hills. Then, during Prohibition, most of the vineyards gave way to other crops.

In 1956, Rose and Leo purchased the 125-acre Sausal Ranch and began planning for their own winery. From her house that was built overlooking the ranch, Rose looked out at a carpet of white prune blossoms that covered much of the valley floor. In the early 1970s, the prunes began to disappear and were replaced by the grape varieties we see today. Fortunately, some of the old Zinfandel vines (a block on the Sausal Ranch dates prior to 1877) survived through all of these transitions and continue to produce to this day. They became the flagship of Sausal Winery, opened by Rose's four children in 1973.

Rose's life evokes the best traditions of Alexander Valley agriculture and winegrowing. After watching the seasons change in the valley for 60 years, Rose has seen crops, wineries, families, and priorities come and go. One thing she is sure of, though: there is no place as unique and beautiful as the Alexander Valley.

Rose Demostene Benson

An Alexander Valley Pioneer

Robert Young

Robert A. Young, a third-generation resident and native of Alexander Valley, was born March 16, 1919. The family ranch had been purchased by Robert's great-grandfather, Peter Young, along with brothers Michael and George, around 1885, after a stint in the gold fields in El Dorado County. The previous owner, Charles McPherson, had purchased the property from the family of Cyrus Alexander, the original land grant owner.

Like many of his contemporaries, Robert Young grew prunes and raised cattle. So how did he get into the vineyard business? In 1962 his farm advisor from the county agricultural extension visited and said, "Why don't you get into grapes?" Robert replied, "But I don't know anything about grapes." The advisor then insisted, "I want you to plant grapes on the back hay pasture." (Not too subtle, that farm advisor!) So, in 1963, the first of Robert Young's vineyards was planted with 14 acres of Cabernet Sauvignon.

It looks like Robert figured out how to grow grapes. In 1975, Dick Arrowood, then the winemaker at Chateau St. Jean Winery, put "Robert Young Vineyard" on the labels of the Chardonnay made exclusively from grapes grown at Robert Young's Alexander Valley ranch. That was the first time a California wine had been given a vineyard designation. The tradition continues as the Robert Young Vineyard Chardonnay still heads the lineup of fine Chardonnay bottlings from Chateau St. Jean.

Today, Robert and his sons, Jim and Fred, farm over 350 acres of premium wine vineyards. In addition to selling grapes to several premium wineries in Sonoma and Napa counties, the Young family has started its own winery—the Robert Young Estate Winery. The endeavor, begun in 1997, involves Robert, his two sons, as well as daughters JoAnn and Susan.

Robert Young has been involved in numerous viticulture, civic and social organizations. His contributions to the community and to winegrowing are respected and valued. He is truly a gentleman and a great resource to Alexander Valley.

Robert Young

The Alexander Valley—Its Beginning . . .

Cyrus Alexander, B. March 15, 1805—D. December 27, 1872, age 67

All information on Cyrus Alexander comes to us from an account written by his nephew Charles, who lived with the Alexander family from 1850 until 1852.

Cyrus left his home in Illinois in the spring of 1831 at the age of 26, after having worked for two of his brothers: first, for William as a tanner where he learned to make shoes; then for brother Hugh, who owned and ran a small tread power mill. Both trades proved of great value when he reached California.

He made his way to the Rocky Mountains where he worked as a fur trapper for the Sublette Fur Company. By 1833 Cyrus had given that up and headed for San Diego where he met Henry Fitch.

Fitch had come to California in 1826, married a Mexican citizen, becoming wealthy in land and cattle. He had a large trade in the hide and tallow business, carried on between San Diego and Boston. By 1837, Cyrus was working for Henry Fitch, and in 1840 was sent north to scout for unclaimed land for which Henry Fitch could apply to the Mexican government.

From San Francisco, Cyrus rode north through the Napa Valley, finding it claimed by George Yount and Edward Bale. Knights' Valley had a few settlers and so he followed an Indian trail west through the hills into an open and fertile valley, rich with water, game and grass, occupied only by Indians. He crossed the Russian River to further explore the lands on the southern side and found more unclaimed land with rich timber, grass and water. Fitch came up to investigate, applied to Mexico for the land and received the grant on September 29, 1841 of the Rancho Sotoyome, 48,800 acres.

Alexander managed this land for Fitch for four years (1840–1844), receiving a two-league portion (8,800 acres) as payment. He built a house for Fitch. Alexander left Fitch's employ in October 1845 and moved to the valley he had chosen as his own, having married Rufena Lucero in December 1844. She was then 14 years old and Alexander was 39.

Cyrus built his first redwood cabin in the Alexander Valley in 1845 but did not receive his official title to the land until September 1847. Plans for a large adobe house were begun and a separate adobe outbuilding was built in which they lived with their first child This building still remains and has been restored and is now the home of Mr. and Mrs. H. Wetzel of Alexander Valley Vineyards.

12

The Alexander Valley Pioneers

The heritage of our valley is being preserved in the form of oral histories by the pioneers who founded it, interviewed by noted author and historian Carol Hicke. This is an ongoing program, sponsored by the Alexander Valley Wine Growers Association, and is maintained at the Sonoma County Wine Library located in the Public Library in Healdsburg. Currently available are:

The Oral Histories of Alexander Valley Pioneers

**"The Seghesio Family, Vineyards and Winery:
One Hundred Years in Alexander Valley"**

**"Grape Growing and Ranching in Alexander Valley:
An Oral History with Maxine and George St. Clair"**

"Rose Demostene: A Life in Alexander Valley Winegrowing"

**"Cuneo and Salal: A Two-Generation Partnership
in Sonoma County Agriculture"**

"Henry Dick: A Lifetime of Agriculture"

"Edwin R. Seberrer: Yesterday & Today in Alexander Valley"

"The Goodyears and the Jimtown Store"

"Robert Young Vineyards: Winegrowing in Alexander Valley"

"Joseph Vercelli: A Wineman for All Seasons"

Alexander Valley Vineyards

Nineteenth-century pioneer Cyrus Alexander explored northern Sonoma County and settled the beautiful valley now named for him, selecting pristine acreage for his own family's estate. More than 100 years later, in 1962, Harry and Maggie Wetzel purchased Alexander's homestead from his heirs. The Wetzel family then became twentieth-century pioneers, as they restored the residence and planted the property with premium grape varieties.

Today the Wetzel Family Estate is home to Alexander Valley Vineyards, a prominent, family-owned and operated vineyard and winery. Grape vines are carefully cultivated on 150 prime acres, reaching from the banks of the Russian River up into the surrounding foothills.

Beginning with Alexander Valley Vineyard's first vintage in 1975, winemaker Hank Wetzel has made estate-grown wines with an owner's dedication. Careful to preserve the quality born in the vineyard, his accomplished efforts have heightened the worldwide reputation of Alexander Valley.

He consistently crafts impressive wines: Chardonnay, Cabernet Sauvignon and Merlot are the principal varietals, along with limited bottlings of Chenin Blanc, Gewürztraminer, Zinfandel, Syrah and Pinot Noir. "My goal is to make wines that capture the exceptional fruit flavors and soft tannins characteristic of this region—wines with accessibility, grace and finesse," he says.

Visitors are welcome at Alexander Valley Vineyards, whether to tour, taste, or purchase wine. The tasting room is open daily, from 10:00 a.m. to 5:00 p.m., except major holidays.

Tours are scheduled by appointment. Picnic tables are available, on a first-come, first-served basis. Come and enjoy the relaxed and beautiful setting.

Chateau Souverain

In 1944, Chateau Souverain founder J. Leland "Lee" Stewart harvested his first crop of wine grapes. He won silver medals at the California State Fair with his first two wines only two years later. Although the names, faces, location, and ownership of the winery have changed, the tradition of fine-wine production remains at Chateau Souverain today.

Chateau Souverain wines continue to win awards and high praise. Winemaker Ed Killian uses only the finest grapes from the best viticultural area for each variety. He makes Cabernet Sauvignon, Merlot, and Sauvignon Blanc wines from grapes from Alexander Valley, the best location for these varieties. Ed's Chardonnay grapes come from the cool-climate viticultural areas of Russian River and Carneros, while his Zinfandel berries come from the location best known for that variety, Dry Creek Valley. You need great fruit to make great wine. This is great fruit.

The winery was built in 1973. A magnificent chateau style, it serves as home to the birth of wonderful wines. Some special, small-production wines are available only at the winery tasting room. These "reserve" wines include Cabernet Sauvignon, Zinfandel, Chardonnay, Viognier, and Syrah. Consistently given high ratings by wine journals, Chateau Souverain wines also earn "best value" ratings year in and year out.

Unique among wineries, Chateau Souverain also offers award-winning cuisine. Opened in 1973 when the winery located in Alexander Valley, the Café at the Winery offers the finest and freshest foods, carefully matched to Ed Killian's wines. Executive chef Martin Courtman, valedictorian at the prestigious Harlow College in Essex, England, has brought fine dining to the Café and wine country since 1991. The wonderful vineyard views from both the dining room and the outside patio further enhance the dining experience.

Chateau Souverain serves up the full package of the Wine Country lifestyle. The great wines, the flavorful food, and the breathtaking views combine to entice visitors back time after time. Come and see (and taste!) for yourself. The winery tasting room is open daily from 10:00 a.m. to 5:00 p.m., except on major holidays. The tasting room may be reached at (707) 857-4245. The Café offers lunch daily from 11:30 a.m. to 2:30 p.m. and dinner Friday through Sunday from 5:30 p.m. to 8:30 p.m. Reservations are strongly recommended. The Café may be reached at (707) 433-3141.

Clos du Bois

America's best-selling producer of Sonoma County wines is celebrating its 27th grape harvest this year. Located between Healdsburg and Geyserville in Sonoma County's Alexander Valley, Clos du Bois was founded in 1974 by Procter & Gamble executive Frank Woods. In two-and-a-half decades, the winery has grown to produce more than one million cases of wine annually and has become one of the most recognizable brand names among wine consumers nationwide.

In 1980, Clos du Bois surprised the wine industry and consumers alike by introducing an affordable barrel-fermented Chardonnay, a wine that today is consistently ranked as one of the top Chardonnays in the country. The winery unveiled a varietal color-coding of each bottle of wine in 1974—yellow for Chardonnay, burgundy red for Cabernet Sauvignon—that quickly became the industry standard. In 1999, Clos du Bois was named one of the country's "Hot Brands" by M. Shanken Communications, publisher of the *Wine Spectator*.

Playing off his last name, founder Woods bestowed the distinctly French name on the fledgling wine company that literally means "enclosure in the wood." Despite their best efforts, consumers often have had difficulty pronouncing *C-L-O D-E-W B-W-A-H*. A recent Clos du Bois radio and print advertising campaign plays on the difficulty of pronouncing the French name in a series of humorous ads. The ads earned Clos du Bois top honors as a finalist for "Regional Marketer of the Year, 1999" at the American Marketing Association Awards held in San Francisco this year.

Over the years, Clos du Bois crushed grapes in several locations—first, near the Alexander Valley Hall on Hwy. 128, then moving to Dry Creek Valley in 1977. In 1979, the operation was located on Mill Street in Healdsburg, and a popular tasting room was opened on Fitch Street in 1984.

A new state-of-the-art winery and tasting room was built at Clos du Bois' present location on Geyserville Avenue in 1990. To keep up with the growth, additions of a 100,000-square-foot barrel room and new bottling lines were completed in time for the 1999 harvest.

"My first job was frost patrol in Frank Woods' Dry Creek vineyard in 1973," says Tom Hobart, the winery's longtime General Manager and the first Clos du Bois employee. "In those days, the Dry Creek Valley was planted mainly in prunes and apples. Grapes were the exception." Needless to say, Hobart stuck with grapes and eventually made the transition to making wine by becoming Clos du Bois' first General Manager in 1980.

In 1988, Frank Woods and his partners sold Clos du Bois to Hiram Walker/Allied Lyons, Plc., which then established a new company in Healdsburg called The Wine Alliance. The Wine Alliance became the sales and marketing "umbrella" for its newly expanding wine division. In 1998, The Wine Alliance became Allied Domecq Wines, USA, to reflect the parent corporate ownership.

In addition to Clos du Bois, Allied Domecq Wines, USA, now encompasses nine wine brands, including Callaway Coastal Winery, William Hill Winery, Atlas Peak Vineyards, Harveys sherries, Domecq sherries, Balbi Vineyards, Marques de Arienzo Rioja Spanish wines and Cockburn's ports.

deLorimier Winery

Founded in 1986, the winery is set in the center of our northern Alexander Valley vineyards, allowing us to carefully tend each small vineyard lot from bud break through harvest. With a capacity of 12,000 cases, the winery was constructed with the blending concept in mind: equipped for the production and aging of many small lots. Every care was taken to enable the winemaker to preserve the quality of the grapes and express his craft.

Al and Sandy deLorimier bring an enormous commitment to innovation, individuality, and quality to the winery venture. Alfred, a renowned pediatric surgeon, is a man with an innovator's spirit and an eye to detail. It is his belief that there is always room for learning and improvement. In that spirit, the vineyards were planted not just with varietals, but, using the most modern viticultural information, with specific clones, rootstocks, and on different trellising schemes. Sandy lends her creativity to build the image of the winery project, developing the proprietary names and innovative label design.

Don Frazer became deLorimier's winemaker in 1989, bringing with him an extensive background in viticulture and winemaking. Don grew up on a family farm north of Sacramento and attended U.C. Davis where he received a degree in Plant Science. In 1978, he joined Charles Krug where he became winemaker in 1980. In 1982, Don accepted a position as winemaker at Belvedere Winery.

Don's winemaking philosophy is that wine is a fruit product and therefore should reflect the varietal character of the grapes as well as the region and vineyard in which they are grown. It is the role of the winemaker to be the guardian of the fruit.

For a wine to be labeled as a varietal, it must be at least 75% of that particular grape. Often, however, the best wine results from a blend of varietals in which the dominant grape is less than 75% of the blend. American wine producers have long been reliant on varietally labeled wines, while in Europe wines are designated by their place of origin. In that spirit, it is the quest of deLorimier Winery to produce wines known more for the character of the estate than for their varietal content.

It has long been their belief that a well-crafted blend will always exceed a single varietal in complexity and overall quality. After more than 20 years of growing grapes on their property in the Alexander Valley, it was time for this belief in the blend to be used to reflect the unique nature of their land.

Field Stone Winery and Vineyard

Conceived and built in 1976 by the late Wallace Johnson, Field Stone remains a family-owned winery and vineyard estate that produces about 10,000 cases of handcrafted wines each year. The viticultural area of our estate is Sonoma County's Alexander Valley, one of America's most celebrated winegrowing regions. Since the late 1960s, when we planted our first modern vineyards, we have been known to such winemakers as André Tchelistcheff, Bill Bonetti, Zelma Long, and Mike Grgich as one of Alexander Valley's premium grape-growing estates. Our Cabernet Sauvignon and Petite Sirah vineyards have set the standard for what many today call the distinctive "Alexander Valley style."

In the early 1960s, following extensive soil and temperature studies, four varietals were chosen from our ranch's experimental test plot: Johannisberg Riesling, Cabernet Sauvignon, Chenin Blanc and Gewürztraminer. In 1966, a planting program of these varieties began, involving only the prime vineyard areas on the ranch—130 acres. Field Stone's fifth variety, the venerable Petite Sirah, comes from an additional 10-acre vineyard on the ranch, planted more than 100 years ago by Italian farmers. This turn-of-the-century vineyard, now thriving in the midst of the new, larger "Terra Rosa" block, was described in the 1895 Alexander Valley Directory as "the best grape land in California."

The winery itself is a unique underground facility carved into a picturesque hillside topped by giant oaks. The name "Field Stone" was derived from the striking rough-hewn entrance facade built of field stones unearthed in 1976. When visiting Field Stone's tasting room, you enter the arched main entrance and wind your way through oak barrels and the enticing smell of aging and fermenting wine. The redwood-paneled tasting room is truly unique, and its service to visitors and customers is the envy of the industry. Since 1987 Field Stone has been selected annually as one of the "Top Ten Tasting Rooms in Napa and Sonoma Counties" from over 200. We are proud of this coveted award and are eager to show each visitor what makes a Field Stone visit so unique and enjoyable.

Conceived as a small estate family winery in the European tradition, each year Field Stone produces select quantities of these red and white varietals: Cabernet Sauvignon, Merlot, Sangiovese, and Old Vine Petite Sirah; Sauvignon Blanc, Chardonnay, Dry Gewürztraminer, and Viognier; and, in some optimal years, a California-style Vintage Petite Sirah Port. Very small quantities of our estate varietals and a non-estate Chardonnay are crafted each year as special *Staten Family Reserve* wines.

Geyser Peak Winery

Geyser Peak Winery was founded in 1880 by one of Sonoma County's pioneer winemakers, Augustus Quitzow. He constructed a winery with a 20,000-gallon capacity on a hillside across from Geyser Peak Mountain in 1882. In 1887, Edward Walden & Company purchased Geyser Peak Winery and 80 acres of vineyards for $10,000. They had been importers of French brandy and were determined to make brandy at Geyser Peak. By 1890, they used 1,800 tons of grapes and made 5,400 gallons of brandy, some of which was exported to Europe.

By 1908 O.J. LeBaron and W.S. Kelly operated the winery under the name Geyser Peak. By 1910 the Ciocca Lombardi Wine Company of San Francisco took over. They expanded the winery and made it one of the largest and best equipped in the entire state.

In 1937, Italy Industries, founded by the Bagnani family took over and Geyser Peak became Redwood Empire Wines. In 1945, Redwood Empire Wines ceased operation and American Industries continued the production of bulk wines at Geyser Peak until the Bagnanis sold the winery to the Schlitz Brewery Corporation of Milwaukee in November 1972.

The Schlitz era was one of great expansion. Three brands were created: the Geyser Peak label for varietal wines, the Voltaire brand of intermediately-priced varietals, and Summit for popular-priced generic wines. The emphasis was put on the Summit four-liter bag-in-a-box concept, which grew in a few years over one million cases, making Geyser Peak Winery the ninth largest winery in California.

In 1980, Schlitz Brewery sold Geyser Peak to Stroh's Brewery Company. Stroh's sold the winery and 500 acres of vineyards in the Alexander Valley to the Trione family of Santa Rosa in 1982. The Trione family sold the Summit brand in 1985 in order to concentrate on the older Geyser Peak brand with its superb vineyards. By 1989, Geyser Peak had become one of the top producers in California. In the same year, winemaker Daryl Groom, known for his premium winemaking in Australia, was hired. Later he brought over winemaker Mick Shroeter to help transform Geyser Peak into one of the most highly awarded wineries in the world.

In the summer of 1998, Mr. Trione sold the winery to Jim Beam Brands Co. Geyser Peak's award-winning wines include Sauvignon Blanc, Chardonnay, Cabernet Sauvignon and Shiraz. The wines are varietal-driven and notable for optimal balance and pairability with food.

Wine enthusiasts are welcome to visit from 10:00 a.m. to 5:00 p.m. daily. Picnic facilities are available.

1880

GEYSER PEAK WINERY

Hanna Winery

Hanna Winery was founded in 1985 by Dr. Elias S. Hanna, a world-renowned cardiac surgeon who lives and practices in San Francisco. Dubbed "the fastest hands in the West," Hanna received his training at Tulane University in New Orleans. Today, Hanna serves as Chief of Cardiac Surgery at Marin General Hospital and Salinas Valley Memorial and is Medical Director of the Western Heart Institute of St. Mary's Hospital in San Francisco.

Hanna was born and raised on a farm in a small village in Syria, overlooking the Mediterranean, where his family grew a variety of crops, including grapevines. "After I moved to San Francisco, I was anxious to find a place in the country. I missed the pace of farm life," Dr. Hanna says. For him, a vineyard was second nature. Beginning with 12 acres in the Russian River Valley that he purchased in the 1970s, Hanna began his foray into winemaking with homemade Cabernet Sauvignon. In the mid-eighties, Dr. Hanna hired a winemaker and expanded his vineyard holdings. Today, Hanna owns 600 acres, about 250 of which are planted, split between four different vineyards.

The Home Estate on Occidental Road in the Russian River Valley is Hanna's flagship vineyard, with 25 acres planted to Chardonnay and Pinot Noir. The Home Estate also currently serves as the winery production facility. A tasting room offers a view of the vineyards and a place for visitors to picnic. Guesthouse facilities are available for out-of-town distributors and preferred accounts. Another 60 acres is planted to Sauvignon Blanc, Chardonnay, and Pinot Noir. Hanna's red wines come from the 88-acre Alexander Valley Red Ranch vineyard, planted to Cabernet, Merlot, Syrah, and Zinfandel.

The vineyard is also the site of Hanna's Hospitality Center, and hosts special events, weddings, and a variety of winery functions. With a panoramic view of the Alexander Valley, the Hospitality Center's wrap-around deck is the perfect place to enjoy a glass of one of Hanna's new releases.

The Bismark Ranch Vineyard, high atop the Mayacamas Mountains, is home to plantings of Cabernet, Merlot, Cabernet Franc, Sangiovese, Syrah, Zinfandel, Petit Verdot, and Malbec. "It's like standing on top of the world!" says General Manager and Vice President Christine Hanna. She adds, "The 1997 harvest was the first time we brought the fruit down from the mountain. The level of concentration and intensity in flavor make for some astounding wines."

Christine is the second generation of Hannas involved in the winery. Dr. Hanna's oldest daughter, she has been working for the winery since 1991. "It's so exciting to see the growth of the winery, particularly in the last couple of years. We've really come into our own with better wines, two tasting rooms, and a stronger presence in the market." An active member of the wine community, Christine serves as President of the Sonoma County Wineries Association, in addition to active membership in both the Alexander Valley Winegrowers and Russian River Valley Winegrowers Association. "It's wonderful to be part of something that has such a bright future. With vineyards in such prime locations in Sonoma County and the dedication of the family and our staff, we are truly positioned for success."

Along with the flagship Sauvignon Blanc, Hanna also produces Chardonnay, Pinot Noir, Merlot, and Cabernet Sauvignon, as well as limited production Reserve wines and the newly-introduced wines from the Bismark Ranch.

Johnson's Alexander Valley Wines

If you long to step back in time and discover a small, rustic, family-owned winery, then a visit to Johnson's Alexander Valley Wines is for you. This winery produces estate-bottled premium varietals available only at the tasting room and by mail order.

Winemaking on the property has deep historical roots. The tasting room, a barn dating back to the 1880s, once housed a winery called "Whiten Bros." In the 1950s, James I. Johnson purchased the ranch as a place to retire. Twenty years later, his sons, Jay, Will, and Tom, bought the property from their father and started the winery.

A self-taught winemaker, Tom won numerous awards for his first releases in 1974. He passed the winemaking torch to his daughter Ellen in 1985, and he now acts as the manager of the vineyard.

Special events throughout the year provide great occasions for a visit. On the last Sunday in July, the Johnsons host an Antique Car Day, and in August there is a family picnic. Anytime that you visit, you can hear the winery's restored 1924 Robert Morton theatre pipe organ, originally from the Capitol Theatre in Sacramento. The pipe organ is a favorite feature of private parties at the winery, often accompanying a silent film in a throwback to the days of yesteryear.

Be sure to give a friendly pat to Sophie and Benjamin Basset, the winery's mascots.

Murphy-Goode Estate Winery

If you ask Tim Murphy, Dale Goode, and Dave Ready why they started Murphy-Goode Winery in 1985, the answer is that it just made sense.

Tim and Dale had been growing grapes in the Alexander Valley separately and as partners for some 20 years. Between the Murphy Ranch and the Murphy-Goode Vineyards, they were farming more than 300 acres of prime vineyards in the Alexander Valley—a combination of respected growers and a prized growing region.

By developing their own winery, the growers could control their own destiny from vineyard to bottle to consumer.

"It's a lot more satisfying to complete the cycle," said Tim. Dale commented, "Growing the grapes is half the job, making wine completes the process."

They already knew wine marketer Dave Ready, and it was a short step to the creation of the Murphy Goode and Ready Wine Company.

The first two vintages were made in leased space with consulting winemaker Merry Edwards. In 1987, a new winery was started on Murphy Ranch land on the eastern edge of the valley northeast of Healdsburg, and Christina Benz was named winemaker.

She said all her winemaking "starts from the vineyard. The winery has to reflect its fruit, and we're fortunate to have exceptional resources. And we all work together here since everyone is involved."

Chris likes to view her winemaking as "attentive." She said, "We pay attention to the fruit and the details, but our role isn't to mask what comes from the vineyards but to enhance it."

Today, Murphy-Goode Winery draws on three primary estate vineyards: the 150-acre Murphy-Goode Vineyard planted to Sauvignon Blanc and Chardonnay; the 165-acre Murphy Ranch and other blocks with Sauvignon Blanc, Sauvignon Musque, Chardonnay, and Gewürztraminer on the valley floor and Cabernet Sauvignon and Merlot on the hillsides; and, finally, the River Ranch with 38 acres planted to Cabernet Sauvignon, Merlot, Petit Verdot plus Sauvignon Blanc and Sauvignon Musque. Murphy-Goode also obtains grapes from neighboring vineyards in the Alexander Valley and from Murphy family vineyards in the Alexander and Russian River Valleys.

First known for its Fumé Blanc, Murphy-Goode is now recognized as one of Alexander Valley's best red wine producers as well, with medal-winning Cabernet Sauvignon, Merlot, "Liar's Dice" Zinfandel, and Pinot Noir.

Today, much of the active day-to-day farming is handled by Tim Murphy's sons TJ, Dennis, and Jim, with Jim and Dennis also owning vineyards of their own. The family approach includes Dave's son, Dave Ready, Jr., who is Murphy-Goode's assistant winemaker, and his youngest son, Adam Ready, who is learning the winemaking process as a member of the winery cellar team.

"Our families are dedicated to this; we all love what we're doing," Tim says. "To us, this isn't a lifestyle, it's a life."

The Sausal Winery

The Alexander Valley's oldest winemaking family is now in its third generation. Our family history began in 1901 when our grandfather, Manuele Demostene, an immigrant from Genoa, Italy, began working on a ranch in the Alexander Valley. Shortly thereafter, our other grandfather, Abele Ferrari, came from Italy and founded the Healdsburg Machine Shop, manufacturing the Healdsburg Grape Crusher.

In 1923, during Prohibition, Abele Ferrari bought the Soda Rock Ranch and Winery in the Alexander Valley. After the repeal of Prohibition, he rebuilt the old stone winery and sold wine in gallon jugs to local stores and neighbors, and in bulk to other wineries.

Romance was the start of the second generation in 1936 when Abele Ferrari's daughter, Rose, married Manuele Demostene's son, Leo. They (our father and mother) lived and worked at the Soda Rock Ranch and Winery until 1956, when they purchased the Sausal Ranch, a 125-acre property planted to prunes, apples and zinfandel grapes, also in the Valley.

Our father, Leo, died before seeing his golden dream of a family winery completed. Honoring his memory, we, the third generation, completed construction of the winery in 1973, the year of his death.

Today, more than 25 years later, we are continuing the family legacy of producing exceptional-quality wines that are sensibly priced. Our wines, particularly the Zinfandels, Cabernet Sauvignon, and Sangiovese enjoy national recognition and praise from wine enthusiasts.

About our wines...

Three of our Zinfandel wines are: old, older, oldest.

Vintage Zinfandel is a blend of grapes from vines that average 50 years old, aged in French and oak barrels for a year or longer. This medium-bodied wine contains dark berry fruit flavors that are characteristic of our Zinfandel wines.

Private Reserve Zinfandel is a limited-edition blend, made entirely from grapes from our 85- to 100-year-old vines. Aged in French and American oak barrels for 18 to 20 months, it is medium-bodied with complex flavors and deep intense fruitiness.

Century Vines Zinfandel is an extraordinary wine whose grapes come only from the five acres of vines that were planted prior to 1877. Aged in French and American oak barrels for 20 to 22 months, it is a Port-like wine of intense dark berry, plum, and raisin flavors. In addition to our Zinfandels, we also produce a classic Sangiovese and a fine Cabernet Sauvignon.

We, the third generation of growers and vintners, are proud of our legacy, and share it with you in the wine that we produce.

Dave Demostene, Winemaker and General Manager

Ed Demostene, Vineyard Manager

Peachie Demostene Dunlavy, Tasting Room Manager

Cindy Demostene Martin, Business Manager

Seghesio Family Vineyards

In 1893, young Italian immigrants Edoardo and Angela met while working at the Italian Swiss Colony Winery in northern Sonoma County. It was their dream to start a winery of their own, so in 1895 Edoardo and Angela Seghesio purchased their family home and 56 acres in the Alexander Valley. They planted Zinfandel vines that first year and realized their dream when their winery was completed in 1902.

In the years preceding and following Prohibition, the Seghesio family produced wine for local customers who purchased it at the winery by the gallon. For larger, more distant customers, the family shipped its wine by rail. By the end of World War II, the Seghesio family had became a large, quality producer selling wine to retail customers as well as to other wineries. In 1983, at the encouragement of the younger generation, the family proudly began to bottle its wines under the Seghesio label.

After more than 100 years as growers, the Seghesio family members continue to commit themselves to the production of superior quality estate wines. They have increased their vineyard plantings and have improved the quality of their fruit by limiting crop yields through careful vine management.

Today, Seghesio Family Vineyards encompasses 400 acres of superior vineyard sites. These sites have been chosen by four generations of Seghesio winemakers for their diversity and ability to produce the finest quality grapes. The winery team now includes eight family members from the third, fourth, and fifth generations of Seghesio family.

The family continues to craft wines from the Zinfandel grapes as Edoardo had. Half of the family's acreage is planted to Zinfandel at five different sites. The winery is also known for fine quality Italian varietals including Sangiovese, Barbera, Arneis, and Pinot Grigio.

The winery's flagship wine, Omaggio (*homage* in Italian) is a tribute to founders Edoardo and Angela Seghesio. It is a blend of the finest lots of Barbera, Sangiovese, Merlot, and Cabernet Sauvignon. This wine was first produced in 1995 as a celebration of the first 100 years of Seghesio family winemaking.

The Seghesio Family Vineyards winery and tasting room are located in the historic town of Healdsburg. The winery is open daily for tasting from 10:00 a.m. to 4:30 p.m. The winery may be reached by phone at (707) 433-7764, or on the Worldwide Web at seghesio.com.

Silver Oak Cellars

To make exceptional Cabernets was my winemaker's dream. When Ray Duncan and I started Silver Oak Cellars in 1972, my dream began to materialize. Now, after 28 exhilarating years, I still get excited every time that crush time rolls around. Over the years we have made many outstanding wines of which I am very proud, but I always remind myself that we have yet to make the perfect Cabernet. The challenge is always out there waiting for the next vintage.

From the start, we have dedicated ourselves to Cabernet. Our wines are produced each year in a time-honored fashion, regardless of vintage or appellation. Our grapes are selected from meticulously farmed vineyards in the Alexander and Napa valleys. Both Cabernets are aged up to 30 months in American oak barrels, and then cellared for another 12 to 18 months, in order to develop the bouquet that comes from lengthy bottle age.

Our extensive aging program, along with a great deal of patience, hard work, and winemaking expertise are responsible for the well-developed bouquet, complexity, and fitness that is Silver Oak's trademark.

All of our first wines, from 1972 through 1978, were from the Alexander Valley. This was the location of our first vineyards. Because these wines have been so consistently delightful, our Alexander Valley Cabernet has become the standard for our finesse-style Cabernet Sauvignons. The interplay of soil and climate in this region produces exquisite wines year after year with only slight vintage variations.

The character of our Alexander Valley Cabernet Sauvignon is exemplified by its softness and drinkability upon release, with more subtle complexity as it matures in the bottle for an additional five to ten years.

In the fall of 1992, we purchased an existing winery in the Alexander Valley, north of Geyserville. We process the grapes from our 200 acres of A.V. vineyards in this state-of-the-art facility. The modified cellar now holds the 4,500 American oak barrels that we need for our extensive aging program.

The airy tasting room and lovely courtyard invite our visitors to relax and enjoy the leisurely pace of Sonoma County, complemented by our great Alexander Valley Cabernets.

Simi Winery

Simi Winery started in 1876 when Guiseppe and Pietro Simi began making wine in San Francisco with Sonoma County grapes. Five years later, they moved their operation to Healdsburg and planted vineyards on the gently rolling hills of Alexander Valley, which reminded them of their native Tuscany. Simi's historic stone cellars were completed in 1890 and are still used to age the winery's fine wines.

One of the many firsts for Simi Winery was the opening of their tasting/retail room in 1934. Just after Prohibition, Isabelle Simi (daughter of Guiseppe) converted a 25,000-gallon champagne barrel into a tasting room located in front of the winery on Healdsburg Avenue. It was a huge success, attracting visitors from around the world. Remodeled in 1970, Simi Winery's tasting room is still a popular stop. With its historic cellars and redwood trees, the winery is a beautiful setting for wine tasting and picnics.

Simi Winery is devoted to producing wines of a place, wines that carry the signature of the land upon which the grapes are grown. Currently, Simi Winery has nearly 500 acres of estate vineyards within the Alexander Valley. These vineyards are planted primarily to red Bordeaux varietals and are the source of Simi's highly allocated Cabernet Sauvignon.

Simi also owns a 100-acre vineyard in the Russian River Valley called the Goldfields Vineyard, which is a great source for Chardonnay fruit to enhance its Sonoma County Chardonnay. This vineyard also produces a single vineyard Chardonnay, Simi Goldfields Vineyard Reserve.

Winemaker Nick Goldschmidt, a charismatic New Zealander who has led Simi's winemaking team since 1990, strives to craft wines that best express the personality and flavors of each site. The result is wines of exceptional balance and finesse that exhibit fine, complex aromas, supple silky textures in the mouth, and long concentrated flavors. Under Nick's supervision, Simi Winery is an innovator of winemaking in Sonoma County, constantly integrating the newest technology and ideas that result in Simi's international reputation of quality and style.

Simi Winery currently produces four wines with the Sonoma County appellation: Cabernet Sauvignon, Chardonnay, Sauvignon Blanc, and Shiraz. Simi also produces Dry Creek Zinfandel and Alexander Valley Merlot. Simi's highly sought after limited production wines include Reserve Cabernet Sauvignon, Goldfields Vineyard Chardonnay, and Sendal, a proprietary blend of Sauvignon Blanc and Sémillon.

Simi's tasting room is open every day from 10:00 a.m. until 5:00 p.m., with regular tours of the facility daily at 11:00 a.m., 1:00 p.m. and 3:00 p.m.

Stonestreet Winery

Near the southern end of Sonoma's Alexander Valley rest 138 acres of pristine vineyards at the base of the slopes of the Mayacamas Mountains. In the fall of 1989, Jess Jackson purchased the property and renamed it in honor of his late father, Jess Stonestreet Jackson. Nestled into a knoll rests the new home of Stonestreet Winery.

In the planning for over a decade, the new Stonestreet Winery is located among existing vineyards just south of Jimtown. The new facility is strategically located a mere five miles from most of the winery's vineyard sources.

More than half of the winery is located underground, with the remaining structures evoking agrarian barns. As Stonestreet General Manager Janet Pagano states, "The new winery was designed to look not only like it belongs here, but to look as if it has been here all along."

The first phase of construction finished just in time to receive the first grapes for the 2000 harvest. Winemaker Michael Westrick says, "We have the advantage now of smaller tanks for keeping small lots separate, a new basket press, and separate barrel rooms for the red and white wines aging in barrels. We now have the ability to hand craft wines with the advantages of modern technology all under one roof."

Stonestreet Winery currently produces approximately 60,000 cases annually, comprised of Cabernet Sauvignon, Merlot, Pinot Noir, Chardonnay, Sauvignon Blanc and a proprietary red blend named Legacy. The winery focuses on Sonoma County fruit, with small lots of single-vineyard wines such as Upper Barn Chardonnay and Christopher's Cabernet Sauvignon, both from the Alexander Mountain Estate.

Stonestreet is recognized as one of California's premier wineries. Over the last decade, the winery earned over eighty Gold Medals and eleven Best-of-Show awards in major judgings across the U.S. and recognition as a Winery of the Year by *Wine and Spirits Magazine* in 1996 and 1998.

The Trentadue Winery

In 1959, Evelyn and Leo Trentadue decided to flee the developers encroaching on their apricot and cherry orchards in Cupertino, the area known today as Silicon Valley. To preserve their way of life, they purchased 208 acres of land in Sonoma County's then remote Alexander Valley.

The Trentadue family were among the very first to plant new vines in Sonoma County since the days of Prohibition. In 1962, the Trentadue family began planting new vines in addition to the 68 acres of old vines already growing on their ranch. Those "new" plantings today are more than 40 years old, and the "old" vines more than 116 years old, making these some of the oldest vineyards in America.

Leo and Evelyn Trentadue are still active owners and continue to expand their winery and vineyards. Recently added to the beautifully manicured winery grounds is a 5,000 sf event center where weddings and other events are hosted throughout the year. A new tasting room and gift shop opened on Healdsburg's plaza. Plans for a new barrel room and visitor center on the winery premises are in the works for the coming year.

Another recent significant change is the appointment of a new winemaker, Miro Tcholakov, a native of Bulgaria. Miro will oversee the winery's production expansion from 9,000 cases to 25,000 cases annually over the next several years.

Family heritage is important to the Trentadues, whose family originally came from the wine-growing regions in Italy. The "32" used throughout the winery refers to the fact that "trente-due," pronounced *tren-tah-doo-ay* in Italian but *tren-tah-doo* here in the U.S., is Italian for the number thirty-two. Family lore has it that 32 families emigrated from France to the town of Bari, Italy. As they remained close to one another in all that they did, they became known as the "32s" or "Trentadue." Leo's family was one of those 32 families.

The winery employs two of Leo's and Evelyn's children, Annette and Victor. Annette is the Purchasing Coordinator assisting with the day-to-day business of the winery. She is often seen in the tasting rooms and in the offices, as well as assisting with the many weddings and special events.

Victor Trentadue is General Manager and Vineyard Manager. He literally grew up among the vines, working in the vineyards after school and during harvest, for as long as he can remember. With the help of wooden blocks attached to the pedals to compensate for his short legs, Victor began driving a tractor at the age of eight. Later, Victor's teenage apprenticeship in the cellar was enough to convince him that viticulture was his true calling. He is responsible for all vineyard and winery operations for the family's winemaking estate.

Today, Trentadue Winery has approximately 100 acres under vine in the Alexander and Dry Creek Valleys. Other than the nine acres planted in Chardonnay, the estate is all red varietals, including Cabernet Sauvignon, Merlot, Sangiovese, Zinfandel, Carignane and Petite Sirah. In addition to the single varietal wines, Trentadue Winery is well known for its gold medal-winning blend of Zinfandel, Carignane and Petite Sirah, called *Old Patch Red*.

The Trentadue Winery is gaining significant recognition for its vintage port wines. Among its medal winners are the 1994 Merlot Port, 1996 Petite Sirah Port and 1996 Wine Port. And, not to be forgotten by anyone who has had the pleasure, is a unique Merlot Port infused with chocolate essence.

White Oak Vineyards and Winery

White Oak Winery is dedicated to producing small quantities of distinguished lots. These wines reflect the uniqueness of the vineyards and climates of this region. Bill Myers, founder, was formerly a building contractor and salmon fisherman in Alaska. During the '70s, Bill was a part-time resident of Healdsburg, trading fresh Alaskan salmon for wine with some of Sonoma County's finest winemakers. With the knowledge from his new friends and a passion for wine, Bill started making wine in his garage. In 1981, Bill decided to open a 2,000-case winery in downtown Healdsburg. Ten years later, White Oak Winery won the Sweepstakes award at the Sonoma County Harvest Fair for its 1990 Chardonnay, competing with 654 entries.

Bill gathered a small group of partners in 1997 to open a new hospitality room and winery in the Alexander Valley. White Oak Winery is now located in 16 glorious acres of old vine Zinfandel and Merlot. White Oak's new winery, designed and hand-built by Bill Myers, is an impressive Mediterranean-style building, complete with a spectacular fountain and exquisite views of Alexander Valley vineyards on Highway 128.

White Oak's winemaker is Steve Ryan, whose philosophy is to let the wines speak for themselves and to make the best possible wines naturally.

White Oak Winery's flagship wines are Chardonnay, with two distinctively different styles; and three Zinfandels, made with grapes from the Alexander Valley estate, Napa Valley, and Mendocino. White Oak also produces Sauvignon Blanc, Merlot, and a Bordeaux-style reserve called Myers Limited Reserve Red. The winery has also recently planted an estate vineyard of Cabernet Sauvignon and Cabernet Franc.

White Oak Winery still has long-term contracts with original grape growers as well as hand-selected new contracts with growers within Sonoma and Napa valleys. These relationships supply Steve with access to some of the highest-quality grapes available. The 10,000 case production of White Oak Winery remains small under Steve's watchful eye to assure the quality care needed to produce his distinguished small lots.

The White Oak Winery hospitality center is open daily from 10:00 a.m. to 5:00 p.m. There is a picnic area with vineyard views located in the courtyard, which may be reserved for groups up to 50 by calling (707) 433-8429.

Hafner Vineyard

Once we saw Alexander Valley, we never looked anywhere else. That was back in 1967 when the valley was filled with prune trees and very few grapes. Early in 1968, we bought a new tractor and began to prepare the ranch for wine grapes. Growing wine grapes was our first love and the hard work of pulling out prune trees and planting grape rootstock really intensified the feeling. Even leafhoppers, mites, vine-nibbling deer, and rattlesnakes didn't discourage us.

Thoughts of a winery began while son Parke pursued his degree in grape growing and winemaking at the University of California Davis. Experience with Louis Martini and Chappellett wineries in Napa Valley was followed by a harvest and crush in France's Burgundy region, and when he returned in late 1981, work on the winery began.

We picked a winery site where vineyards, oak-covered hills, and creek meet. The new building was modeled after a 19th-century winery that once stood nearby, and we had our first crush in autumn 1982. Twelve years later, wine caves were bored into the hills behind the winery for 700 oak barrels to allow more barrel-aging time.

In planning the winery, we agreed we wanted to remain small, sell direct to patrons, focus on Chardonnay and Cabernet, age them longer than most for greater maturity, maintain fair prices, and provide swift, dependable service.

Marketing began in 1984 with the 1982 Chardonnay, and son Scott created our program of direct sale to patrons, quickly earning a reputation for creative, personal service (a real voice on the phone).

In 1985, drawing on his experience in Burgundy, Parke created a second Chardonnay to be released with over three years of age, the Winemaker's Reserve. It is one of only three wines made at Hafner Vineyard and all three are Estate-Bottled, which means they are made only from grapes grown in the vineyard at the winery.

The Reserve Chardonnay is a big, rich wine with a complex bouquet. One hundred percent barrel-fermented, then it is aged in French oak barrels for 15 months before it is given nearly two years of bottle aging.

Our principal Chardonnay is one-third barrel-fermented and two-thirds fermented in temperature-controlled tanks to slow fermenting and retain more of the grape aromas. One-third of this Chardonnay is malolactic-fermented and the entire vintage is given a year in oak before a year of bottle-aging. This wine is youthful, crisp, and aromatic.

The Cabernets of Alexander Valley are softer than those of most Napa Valley districts. Two years in barrels in our caves, followed by two-and-a-half years in bottles, led to their March release at four-and-a-half years of age. The result is a soft wine with firm berry-cherry aromas, a hint of dark, dark chocolate, and, in some years, wisps of cedar and leather. Judging by 19 vintages, our Cabernets add depth and roundness as they age.

A small number of California restaurants whose cuisines are acclaimed nationally offer Hafner wines. Our wines are also available by mail order from the winery, as we do not have tasting room facilities.

Sommer Vineyards Estate Winery

Sommer Vineyards is a small, family-run winery nestled in the heart of the Alexander Valley. The winery was founded in 1974 by the Sommer family, who fell in love with the views of the Mayacamas, Alexander Valley vineyards and the Russian River from the knoll upon which the winery rests.

The Sommers were also attracted by the untouched beauty of Alexander Valley—still one of the last outposts in the wine country to experience a quieter, friendlier, more intimate place for farming and vinifying fine wines. Despite the world-class wines made here—we still know our neighbors, and everyone has a warm hello for visitors.

The estate winery rests on 32 acres, planted to Cabernet, 75-year-old Zinfandel vines, and Merlot. Our good neighbors, the Fanucchis, grow our Sangiovese, and the Osbornes, on the next ranch, graciously supplied the grapes for our Late Harvest Sémillon. From the beginning, it was the family's dream to make exceptional wines that were true to the character of Alexander Valley, and wines that they themselves loved to drink—wines with full, lush fruit and balanced structure to pair well with their favorite foods.

Stuhlmuller Vineyards

Stuhlmuller Vineyards, located just outside the town of Healdsburg, is a family-owned vineyard and winery near the end of West Soda Rock Lane. They are in the southernmost reaches of the Alexander Valley where the hills meet the Russian River, and where fruit maturity can be pushed to the limit without sacrificing quality, owing to the coolness of the nights in the region.

Carmen and Roger purchased the original vineyard in 1982. Since then, the vineyards have grown to 160 acres of hillside and bench plantings of Chardonnay and Cabernet Sauvignon. The Chardonnay scion wood was selected from the notable "Upper Barn" Chardonnay vineyard of the Gaur Ranch. Bud wood from the Belle Terre Vineyard was used for the Cabernet.

In 1996, Fritz Stuhlmuller, the oldest of the next generation of Stuhlmullers, produced a tiny amount of Chardonnay. The result was a concentrated and dense wine that, because of the cool micro-climate on West Soda Rock Lane, exhibited a brightness of life and dimension. The wine was a hit on both coasts. Fritz was on his way and taking his family with him.

Anticipating vintage 2000, an original, early century barn on the property will be converted to a small facility under the direction of Winemaker Kerry Damskey and Vineyard Manager and Assistant Winemaker Dave Collin.

The style of wines, as defined by Kerry, will be that of concentrated flavors with the unique expression of the vineyard's hillside and benchland terroir. A super premium-level Chardonnay and a Bordeaux blend style of Cabernet Sauvignon.

While Roger and Carmen will continue to sell their grapes to some of Sonoma County's most notable wine producers, Fritz will concentrate on limited quantities of hand-crafted and estate-grown wines.

There is a proverb that tells us, "The best fertilizer in the vineyard is the owner's footprint." Owned by our family since 1982, Stuhlmuller Vineyards is located in the coastal cool of the Alexander Valley, along the Russian River. An old oak tree that overlooks our vineyard has become symbolic of the freedom, joy, and family life that the Stuhlmuller Vineyards property has come to represent. Under this tree is a picnic bench with a plaque dedicated to a family friend that reads, "Steve's Spot. May it always be shared." That tree and bench are shared with you on our label.

The Jimtown Store—An Alexander Valley Landmark

In the early days of the Alexander Valley, pioneers Bob and Caroline Goodyear ran the Jimtown store. Bob's father, Lloyd Goodyear, had purchased the property in 1930. The store then served as a focal point for local residents, selling the unusual array of goods from chicken food to beer. It also functioned as a bank to many by cashing checks and selling money orders.

Farmworkers were a mainstay at the store during the Goodyears' ownership. Caroline, fluent in Spanish, helped many with their government paperwork such as driver's license renewals. Running a "tab" was a common practice at the store where payday became the time when cash changed hands.

By 1984, Bob and Caroline decided to sell the store and retire. Large supermarkets had cut into their business and long hours had taken their toll. The sale left a void in both merchandise and personalities in the valley.

Then in 1989, former Silver Palate partner John Werner and his wife, artist Carrie Brown, chanced upon the store while visiting from New York City. Soon after learning it was for sale, the couple bought Jimtown. They had been looking for a business opportunity that would combine their interests and immediately set out to revive the abandoned landmark to its former glory—and add a few twists of their own.

Jimtown is actually a compound spread out over an acre. The property now includes a large general store, a renovated migrant worker's cottage designed by noted San Francisco architects Richard Fernau and Laura Hartman, and barns used as storage for antiques.

Werner and Brown have fashioned Jimtown into a celebration of Americana. Publications, including *USA Today*, the *New York Times* and *HG*, have written enthusiastically about this culinary oasis tucked away in a small corner of Alexander Valley. Those in the know arrive anxious for Jimtown's hearty well-prepared food, premium wine from top Sonoma County vintners, and distinctive antiques and collectibles. Brown and Werner are admirers of vintage Americana and have traveled widely to assemble an eclectic collection for themselves, including a running 1955 red Ford pickup that for years served as a county fire truck.

They have carefully built a business that comfortably accommodates both tourists and the local population that has traditionally supported the Jimtown Store. Look past the deli counter featuring distinctive gourmet food items made from locally-grown produce and one will encounter the important everyday necessities that any country general store worth its salt carries, everything from bleach to toy planes.

Located at 6706 State Hwy. 128 in Healdsburg, California, 70 miles north of the Golden Gate in Alexander Valley. The store hours are 7:00 a.m. to 5:00 p.m., Monday through Friday, and 7:30 a.m. to 5:30 p.m., Saturday and Sunday.

The Jimtown Store features homemade foods, groceries and sundried, regional and local food and wine, picnic lunches and supplies, catering service, antiques, and gifts. Their website and online catalogue are at www.jimtown.com.

Jimtown Store began developing their line of fresh condiments in 1991. The Olive Salad was such a success, it was followed by Chickpea Chipotle Spread, Fire Roasted Vegetables, Fig & Olive Tapenade, Romesco Spread, and "Go-Thai" Peanut Dip'n Sauce.

JIMTOWN STORE

6706

ANTIQUES

Homemade
GOOD FOOD
ESPRESSO
LOCAL PRODUC

od Coffee & Real Food

ALEXANDER VALLEY WINEGROWERS

JIMTOWN STORE

Spring Recipes

Roasted Garlic Vichyssoise

5 cups chicken stock
5 russet potatoes, peeled and sliced
2 large leeks, white part only, sliced
*   and cleaned*
2 stalks celery, sliced
1 large onion, roughly chopped
1 large head garlic, sliced 1/4 inch
*   across top*

Olive oil
1 pint half-and-half
Salt
White pepper
1/2 bunch chives, thinly sliced with
*   some left whole for garnish*

Place chicken stock in large pan, add vegetables to chicken stock and simmer about 45 minutes until tender; let cool slightly. Drizzle garlic head with olive oil and bake garlic head in oven at 325 degrees for an hour, or until soft and fragrant. Add soft, cooked garlic cloves to soup stock. Purée all in the blender. When completely cooled, add half-and-half, salt, pepper, and finely minced chives. Garnish with whole chives.

Serves 6 to 8.

Serve with Murphy-Goode Reserve Fumé or "Liar's Dice" Zinfandel.

Murphy-Goode Estate Winery

Cream of Mushroom Soup

1 pound onions, diced
3 tablespoons fresh garlic, chopped
1 pound butter
4 pounds mushrooms, chopped
1 bay leaf

Salt and pepper
1 gallon chicken stock
1 quart cream or half-and-half
4 tablespoons toasted almonds

Sauté onions, garlic and butter until onions are limp. Add mushrooms, bay leaf, salt, pepper, and chicken stock. Cook at least one hour. Remove bay leaf. Add cream and almonds.

Tighten with roux if necessary. (Roux is equal parts of melted butter and flour.) Cook 7 minutes. Warm. Add a small amount of warm soup to roux mixture, mix well, then add to balance of soup, stirring carefully to prevent lumping. Serve with salad and a simple bread.

Serves 24.

This is a very rich soup.

Serve with Merlot or Pinot Noir.

Vail Vista Vineyard

Chicken Soup with Mushrooms and Wild Rice

2/3 cup wild rice
2-1/4 teaspoon salt
5 cups water
2 tablespoons olive oil
1 medium onion, coarsely chopped
2 carrots, sliced
2 ribs celery, chopped
2 cloves garlic, minced
9 cups chicken stock
4 teaspoons thyme, chopped, or
  1-1/2 teaspoons dried)

1/2 teaspoon dried sage
2 cups cooked chicken, cubed
6 ounces mushrooms, thinly sliced
1/4 teaspoon freshly ground black
  pepper
2 tablespoons fresh chives, chopped
  (or green onion tops, minced)
2 tablespoons chopped fresh cilantro
1/4 cup White Oak Chardonnay

In a saucepan, combine the rice, 1/4 teaspoon salt and the water. Bring to a boil, reduce heat, cover and simmer until the rice is tender, about 40 minutes.

In a large pot, heat the oil. Add the onion, carrots, celery and garlic and cook until the onion is translucent. Add the stock, spices and salt, and bring to a boil. Reduce heat and simmer 5 minutes. Add the cooked rice, chicken, mushrooms, and pepper and simmer until the vegetables are done. Serve topped with chives and cilantro.

Serves 6.

Serve with White Oak Chardonnay.

White Oaks Vineyards and Winery

Mexican Chicken Casserole

1 (10-3/4-ounce) can cream of
   mushroom soup
2/3 cup milk
1/2 teaspoon salt
1 cup cream-style cottage cheese
6 ounces cream cheese, crumbled
1/2 teaspoon poultry seasoning
1/3 cup chopped onion
1 (4-ounce) can mild green chilies,
   chopped

3 cups cooked chicken, diced
1 (6-3/4-ounce) bag Doritos or taco-
   flavored corn chips
2 cups grated mild Cheddar cheese
1/4 to 1/3 cup grated Parmesan cheese
Bread crumbs
Pimiento strips (optional)

Preheat oven to 350 degrees. Heat together soup, milk and salt. Stir in cottage cheese and cream cheese. Add poultry seasoning, onion, chilies and chicken.

In a casserole, layer the corn chips, chicken mixture and the Cheddar cheese. Repeat. Sprinkle top with Parmesan cheese and bread crumbs. Garnish with pimiento. Bake for 30 minutes.

Serves 8.

Easy to double or triple this recipe.

Serve with Chateau Souverain 1996 Stuhlmuller Vineyards Cabernet.

Stuhlmuller Vineyards

Lupe's Tomatillo Salsa

1 pound tomatillos
2 to 3 serrano chilies
3/4 cup whole cilantro leaves
3/4 cup chopped cilantro
1 clove garlic, minced
1 tablespoon + 1 teaspoon yellow
*   onion, finely chopped*

2 tablespoons scallions, finely
*   chopped*
Salt to taste
1 to 2 teaspoons sugar optional—to
*   taste*

Remove the stems and papery outer husks from the tomatillos. With a sharp paring knife, remove the stem "eyes." Snap off the stems from the serrano chilies. Fill a medium-sized pot three-quarters full with water and bring it to a boil. Add the tomatillos and serranos and reduce the flame to low. Simmer, uncovered, stirring occasionally, for 10 minutes.

Drain and cool the tomatillos and serranos. Place 3/4 cup of cilantro leaves in a blender (reserve the remaining 3/4 cup and chop finely). Add the garlic, yellow onion, cooled tomatillos, and serranos. Purée on low for 30 seconds and scrape down the insides of the blender container. Repeat until smooth.

Pour the salsa into a bowl; add the scallions and chopped cilantro. Salt to taste. If the salsa seems too bitter or tart, add a little sugar to taste.

                                    Makes approximately 2 cups.

© *Jimtown Store 2000*

Jimtown Store

Goat Cheese Ravioli
with Roasted Red Jalapeño Sauce

4 ounces goat cheese
2 ounces Ricotta cheese
2 ounces Parmesan cheese, grated
6 ounces potato purée
2 eggs
2 tablespoons chopped fresh herbs
(Italian parsley, tarragon, oregano)

2 tablespoons chopped chives
1 pound (approximately 6) pasta
sheets*
Salt and freshly ground pepper to
taste

Place the cheeses, eggs, and mixed herbs (except chives) in a food processor and combine. Add potato purée and seasonings, then combine just enough to mix thoroughly (do not mix too long). Pour mixture into a bowl and fold in chives.

To make the ravioli, lightly dust your work surface with semolina flour. Cut the pasta sheets into 5-inch x 30-inch rectangles. Brush the bottom half of the dough with egg wash and, using a heaping teaspoon of filling, spoon into mounds onto dough, about 2-1/2 inches apart. Fold over the top half of the dough to cover the mounds and, using your fingers, firmly press around the mounds to seal the two sides. With a 2-1/2-inch round cookie cutter, cut out the ravioli and place on a tray that has been dusted with semolina flour. (May be made ahead of time and kept in refrigerator until needed.) To cook, place in boiling salted water for about 4 to 5 minutes. Makes 20 ravioli.

*(May be purchased at a gourmet food store or made fresh. Try using a flavored variety such as herb or tomato.)

Roasted Red Jalapeño Sauce

2 tablespoons chopped shallots
4 whole peeled garlic cloves
3/4 cup Chateau Souverain Chardonnay
3 cups heavy cream
2 ounces butter
1 tablespoon roasted red jalapeño purée

2 tablespoons roasted red bell pepper
  purée
Cayenne pepper
Salt and freshly ground black pepper
  to taste

In 1 ounce of butter, sauté the shallots and garlic cloves in a saucepan, being careful not to color them. Add the Chardonnay and reduce slowly by two-thirds, add the cream and reduce by one-third, and add the two purées and seasonings. Transfer sauce to a blender and purée. Strain sauce and then finish with the remaining butter. Makes 2-1/2 cups.

Serve the ravioli with the hot roasted red jalapeño sauce.

Serves 4.

Recipe by Martin W. Courtman, Executive Chef, Chateau Souverain.

Serve with Chateau Souverain Reserve Zinfandel.

Chateau Souverain

Warm Goat Cheese Flan
with Sweet Red Pepper Sauce

3 red peppers	*2 egg yolks*
2 tablespoons virgin olive oil	*1/2 cup whipping cream, reduced to*
1 pound fresh goat cheese	*1/4 cup*
1 egg	*Salt and pepper*

For sauce: Cut peppers in half. Remove seeds and ribs. Rub with a little olive oil and roast in a 450-degree oven for about 30 minutes, until skin blisters. Put in paper bag to steam. When cool, remove skin. Purée in food processor with the extra virgin olive oil. This can be made a day or two ahead and stores in refrigerator.

For flan: Purée cheese and eggs in food processor until smooth. With motor running, add the reduced cream. Scrape sides of bowl. Add a little salt and pepper. Butter 8 small ramekins and divide the cheese mix. Cover each with aluminum foil. Bake in pan with a water bath (about 1-1/2 inches of water) at 350 degrees for 25 to 30 minutes, until firm. Invert onto plate. Serve sauce around the flan.

Serves 8.

Serve with Hafner Cabernet Sauvignon.

Hafner Vineyard

Bowtie Pasta with Lamb, Pine Nuts and Mascarpone Cream Sauce

1 tablespoon Hanna olive oil
1 shallot, peeled and minced
1 pint heavy cream
1 sprig rosemary
4 ounces Mascarpone cheese
1 pound lamb loin, boned and
  trimmed
Salt and pepper to taste

1 clove garlic, peeled and mashed
12 ounces dried bowtie pasta
1/2 cup pine nuts, toasted
Grated Asiago cheese to taste
Rosemary sprigs for garnish

For the sauce: heat the oil in a small pan over medium-high heat. Add the shallots and sauté until softened and translucent. Add the cream and rosemary sprig and bring to a boil. Reduce the heat to low and simmer until the volume is reduced by half. Remove from heat, add the Mascarpone and whisk until incorporated. Discard the rosemary sprig, season and set aside, keeping warm.

For the lamb, preheat oven to 400 degrees. Season lamb with salt and pepper, rub with garlic and place on a sheet pan or broiler pan. Set in the oven and roast for 20 minutes, or to desired doneness. Remove from the oven and set aside to rest for 10 minutes before slicing.

In a large pot of boiling salted water, add the pasta and cook until tender, strain and return to the pan. Slice the lamb into rounds 1/4-inch thick and add to pasta. Add the sauce and toss until pasta is evenly coated. To serve, spoon the pasta into a bowl, sprinkle with pine nuts, and serve with grated Asiago cheese. Garnish with a sprig of rosemary.

Serves 4.

Serve with Hanna Alexander Valley Merlot.

Hanna Winery

Asparagus and Prosciutto Rolls

24 spears medium asparagus
8 thin (but not paper-thin) slices
  prosciutto
1 small head frisée or curly endive

Lemon oil
Freshly ground black pepper
Optional: Parmesan shavings

Snap off the tough ends of the asparagus and trim spears to even lengths. Cook in boiling, salted water for 6 to 7 minutes, or until asparagus is bright green and crisp-tender. Lift out with tongs and let drain and cool to room temperature.

Arrange a bundle of 3 spears of asparagus lengthwise on a slice of prosciutto and roll up. Cut horizontally into 4 or 5 even pieces. Stand on end and tuck a sprig of frisée or curly endive into the top of each piece. Sprinkle tops with a little lemon oil and a grinding of black pepper.

For a plated first course, cut the bundles into uneven lengths for visual interest and stand a group in the middle of a plate. You can be a little more generous with the lemon oil and scatter Parmesan shavings over the top.

Serves 4 to 6 as a first course,
or makes 32 to 40 pieces for hors d'oeuvres

© Mary Evely, Executive Chef, Simi Winery

Serve with Simi Sauvignon Blanc.

Simi Winery

Avocado and Pear Salad with Smoked Chicken

1 firm ripe pear
Juice of 1/4 lemon
1 shallot, minced
1 teaspoon snipped chives
2 tablespoons pear or Champagne
  vinegar
3 tablespoons hazelnut oil
3 tablespoons peanut oil
Kosher salt

Black pepper in a mill
2 cups arugula leaves
1 ripe Haas avocado, pitted and cut
  lengthwise into 1/8-inch slices
4 ounces (about 1 cup) smoked chicken
  meat, cut into medium julienne
1/4 cup hazelnuts, toasted lightly and
  skinned

Peel the pear, core it, and cut it lengthwise into 1/8-inch-thick slices. Place the slices in a small bowl, cover them with cold water, and add the lemon juice to keep them from browning. Set the bowl aside.

In a small bowl, whisk together the shallot, chives, vinegar, and hazelnut and peanut oils. Taste, and season with salt and pepper. In a separate bowl, toss the arugula with half of the dressing. Place the dressed arugula in the center of each of 4 salad plates. Arrange the pear and avocado slices around the arugula, and divide the chicken among the portions, placing it on top of the arugula. Spoon the remaining dressing over the salads, scatter a few hazelnuts over each one, and serve immediately.

Serves 4.

Recipe © Michele Anna Jordan

Serve with 1999 Clos du Bois Alexander Valley Reserve Chardonnay.

Clos du Bois Winery

Rabbit Cacciatore Lombard Style

*2 full rabbit breasts, cleaved in two
   and hacked crosswise for 8 pieces*
4 rabbit thighs
1 tablespoon olive oil
16 ounces chicken stock
1/2 medium onion, chopped finely
1 carrot, chopped finely
1 celery stock, chopped finely

2 large sprigs of rosemary
*8 ounces criminni or button
   mushrooms (if large, cut in half)*
6 ounces Trentadue Merlot
Salt and pepper to taste
*Arrowroot or cornstarch for
   thickening, if desired*

In a large, heavy skillet or cast iron Dutch oven bottom, brown the rabbit pieces in the oil. Add the finely chopped onion, carrot, and celery and sauté until the onions are translucent. Add the rosemary and chicken stock to almost cover the rabbit pieces and simmer for 30 minutes, or until the rabbit is cooked through. Add the mushrooms and simmer for another 10 to 15 minutes until the mushrooms have shrunk slightly in size. Add the Trentadue Merlot and continue to simmer for another 5 minutes. Salt and pepper to taste. If desired, stir in the arrowroot or cornstarch to thicken slightly.

Serves 4.

Recipe by Don Bodio, Trentadue Winery.

This cacciatore may be made with chicken as a substitute for rabbit. At my Nonna's home, she served it over soft polenta with gorgonzola.

Serve with Trentadue 1996 Alexander Valley Merlot.

Trentadue Winery

Spring Tuna Stir Fry

1 pound Ahi tuna steaks
2 tablespoons olive oil
1/4 teaspoon Five Spice
1 large red or yellow pepper
1 large onion, sliced thin

1 bunch asparagus, preferably very
* skinny, sliced in 1-1/2 to 2-inch pieces*
2 tablespoons toasted sesame seed oil
1/2 tablespoon hot chili oil
3 tablespoons soy sauce

Coat tuna with olive oil and sprinkle on Five Spice. Grill on barbecue until done medium. Allow to cool. Crumble into small pieces.

Stir fry asparagus, pepper and onion in the oils. When still crunchy but cooked, add the tuna and soy sauce and toss until all ingredients are coated with oil and soy sauce. Serve either hot or refrigerated (best for a warm spring day) over fresh pepper linguine. Add soy sauce to taste.

Serves 4.

Serve with Chateau Souverain Reserve Chardonnay.

Chalk's Bend Vineyard

Risotto Primavera

3 tablespoons butter
1/4 cup sliced shallots
1-1/2 cups Arborio rice (Italian short
  grain)
3/4 cup sliced shiitake mushrooms
1-1/2 tablespoons chopped, roasted
  garlic cloves
1/2 cup dry white wine
5 to 6 cups chicken stock (2-1/2 cans)

1/2 cup freshly grated Parmesan or
  Asiago cheese
2 teaspoons grated lemon zest
1 cup thinly sliced young asparagus,
  stalks trimmed, cut on the diagonal
1/4 cup minced fresh chives
Salt
Freshly ground black pepper

Melt butter in a medium saucepan. Add shallots and cook over moderate heat until soft, not brown. Add rice and shiitake mushrooms, cooking evenly until rice is translucent, about 3 minutes. Add garlic, wine and 4 ounces (1/2 cup) of stock and cook, stirring constantly, until liquid is absorbed. Continue adding 1/2 cup amounts of stock and cooking in this manner until rice is creamy but center is firm, 15 or more minutes (taste to check).

When rice is done, stir in cheese, lemon zest, asparagus, and chives. Salt and pepper to taste. Serve in warm bowls garnished with shaved Parmesan and fresh basil sprigs.

Serves 6.

Serve with Sausal Sangiovese.

Sausal Winery

Salmon, Asparagus and Roasted New Potatoes

*1 pound small new potatoes, washed
  and halved*
2 tablespoons olive oil
*1/2 pound medium asparagus,
  trimmed and sliced on diagonal,
  1/2-inch thick*
*1 tablespoon chopped fresh dill plus
  dill sprigs for garnish*

1 strip lemon zest (1/2 by 2 inches)
1 small garlic clove, coarsely chopped
1/2 teaspoon salt
Freshly ground pepper
*2 salmon steaks (10 ounces each), cut
  about 1-inch thick*
1 lemon, cut into large wedges

Preheat oven to 400 degrees. In a large, shallow baking dish (about 10 x 14 inches), toss the potatoes with olive oil. Arrange the potatoes, cut sides down, in the baking dish and roast for 10 to 12 minutes, or until the potatoes begin to brown on the bottom. Turn the potatoes over and roast for 10 minutes longer, or until browned on top. Remove baking dish from oven.

In a medium bowl, toss the asparagus with the chopped dill, lemon zest, garlic, salt, and season with pepper to taste. Add the asparagus mixture to the potatoes and stir to combine.

Push the vegetables to the sides of the dish and arrange salmon steaks in center. Return the baking dish to the oven and roast 10 to 12 minutes, or until fish is cooked through.

Spoon vegetables onto 4 warmed plates. Remove salmon skin and center bone from each steak. Place divided steaks onto the plates and squeeze one lemon wedge over them. Garnish with dill sprigs and lemon wedges.

Serves 4.

Serve with deLorimier "Spectrum."

deLorimier Winery

Chicken Parmesan

4 boneless chicken breasts
1 large yellow onion, chopped
3 cloves garlic, minced
16 oz. can chopped tomatoes
1 cup white wine

1 teaspoon oregano
Salt and Pepper to taste
4 thick slices of teleme cheese
Fresh grated Parmesan cheese
Olive oil

Pound chicken breasts with a mallet or the side of a meat cleaver until flat. Dredge in flour, salt and pepper. B rown in oil, set aside.

Chop and sauté onion, add garlic and tomatoes. Simmer briefly before adding white wine, oregano, and salt and pepper. Pour 2/3 of sauce in baking dish, placing browned chicken breasts on the sauce and top each chicken breadt with a slice of the teleme cheese. Cover with remaining sauce. Sprinkle with the fresh Parmesan cheese and bake at 350 degrees for 30 minutes. Serve fresh Parmasan at table.

Serves 4.

Pour Silver Oak Cellars Cabernet Sauvignon.

Silver Oak Cellars

Risotto Milanese

3-1/2 cups chicken stock
2 tablespoons olive oil
2 tablespoons butter
1 yellow onion, chopped
1 cup Arborio rice
1/2 cup Seghesio ARNEIS wine
1 clove garlic, minced

1 ounce dried porcini mushrooms,
  rehydrated in 1/4 cup stock
1/4 teaspoon saffron
1/4 to 1/2 cup freshly grated
  Parmesan cheese
Freshly ground pepper to taste

Simmer chicken stock in separate pan. Sauté onion in olive oil and butter in a large skillet until onion is clear. Add rice to onion, sautéing for 5 minutes. (It is important to stir constantly from the time the rice is added until the rice is tender.) Add wine and garlic to mixture and allow liquid to cook down. Then add 1/2 cup of warm stock and rehydrated mushrooms with their liquid. Allow liquid to cook down.

As the liquid simmers away, continue adding 1/2 cup of warm stock. Repeat this process until the rice is tender, approximately 30 minutes. With the last 1/2 cup of stock, add the saffron. When rice is tender, stir in 1/4 to 1/2 cup of Parmesan cheese and freshly ground pepper to taste. Serve immediately.

Serves 2 as a main dish or 4 as a side dish.

From the kitchen of Ed Seghesio.

Serve with Seghesio ARNEIS.

Seghesio Family Vineyards

Spring

Very Fast Spring Salad

1 (10-ounce) bag mixed salad greens
2 large navel oranges, peeled and
    sectioned
1/2 cup Italian dressing

4 ounces crumbled Feta cheese
1 cup seasoned croutons
1 cup chopped walnuts

Arrange salad greens in a large bowl. Drizzle with dressing and top with remaining ingredients. Serve immediately with fresh, cracked pepper.

Serves 4 to 6.

Serve with Field Stone Chardonnay.

Field Stone Winery

Western Hash

1 pound ground beef
1/2 cup chopped onion
3-1/2 cups canned tomatoes
1 cup chopped green pepper

1/2 cup uncooked rice
1/2 teaspoon basil
Garlic salt and pepper to taste
1/2 pound sliced Monterey Jack cheese

Brown ground beef with onions. Add tomatoes, green pepper, rice, basil and other seasonings. Cover and simmer 25 minutes, stirring occasionally.

Transfer mixture to 9 x 9-inch buttered casserole. Top with sliced Monterey Jack cheese. Heat in warm oven until cheese is melted and slightly browned.

Serves 6.

Wasson Vineyards

White Chocolate and Strawberry Cheesecake

1 (9-ounce) package chocolate wafer
   cookies, broken
1/2 cup unsalted butter, melted
1 pound white chocolate, finely
   chopped
4 (8-ounce) packages cream cheese, at
   room temperature
1 cup sugar

1/4 teaspoon salt
4 large eggs
1 cup sour cream
2 tablespoons vanilla extract
3 (1-pint) baskets strawberries, hulled
   and halved
1/2 cup apricot preserves
2 tablespoons Brandy

Preheat oven to 325 degrees. Butter 10-inch spring-form pan and wrap outside of pan with foil. To prepare crust, finely grind cookies in food processor. Add butter and continue to process until crumbs are moist. Press crumbs into bottom of pan and up the sides 2 inches. Bake about 15 minutes. Cool on a rack at room temperature.

Filling: Stir white chocolate in the top of a double boiler, over water in the bottom part of boiler, until melted and smooth. Remove from water and cool until luke-warm, continuously stirring. Beat cream cheese in large bowl using electric mixer until fluffy. Gradually add sugar, then salt and beat until smooth. Add eggs one at a time, beating well after each addition. Add sour cream, whipping cream and vanilla until well blended. Gradually add melted chocolate. Beat until smooth and pour filling into crust.

Bake cake until top begins to brown, but the center still moves when shaken. Turn off oven and open oven door slightly. Leave cake in the oven for another 30 minutes. Remove cake and chill uncovered cake overnight. Remove spring-form sides from cake. Mix Brandy and preserves in heavy saucepan until boiling. Strain preserves. Top cake with fresh strawberries and glaze with Brandy preserve sauce. Chill and serve.

Serves 12 to 14.

Serve with Geyser Peak Riesling.

Geyser Peak Winery

Grilled Swordfish with Thai Red Curry Sauce

1 teaspoon Thai red curry paste
1/2-inch piece fresh ginger, peeled and
* minced*
1 (12-ounce) can coconut milk
1 tablespoon Thai fish sauce (nuac
* nuom) or soy sauce*
1 sprig fresh basil, stemmed and
* chopped*
1 kaffir lime leaf or zest of 1 lime
1 stalk lemon grass, trimmed and
* sliced*

1 teaspoon cornstarch, dissolved in 2
* teaspoons cold water*
1 red bell pepper, stemmed, seeded and
* sliced into strips*
1 green bell pepper, stemmed, seeded
* and sliced into strips*
4 6-ounce swordfish steaks
Juice of 1/2 lime
Salt and pepper to taste

For the curry: In a medium saucepan over medium-high heat, put the curry paste and ginger and sauté for 3 minutes. Reduce the heat to low and add the coconut milk, whisking until incorporated. Add the fish sauce, basil, lime leaf and lemon grass and continue to simmer over low heat for 10 minutes. Strain the sauce into a medium saucepan and bring to a boil over medium-high heat. Incorporate the cornstarch mixture, reduce heat, and simmer until the sauce has thickened. Add the bell peppers and continue cooking until the vegetables have softened slightly. Remove from heat, season and set aside, keeping warm.

Preheat the broiler. Season the swordfish with lime juice, salt and pepper, and arrange on a sheet pan. Place under the broiler and cook for 5 minutes on each side, or to desired doneness. Remove from the oven and set aside.

To serve: Place a piece of swordfish onto a plate, pour some of the sauce and peppers on top and serve with steamed rice.

Serves 4.

Serve with a crisp Hanna Russian River Valley Sauvignon Blanc.

Hanna Winery

Vietnamese Grilled Beef Wrapped in Grape Leaves

*1 pound Chateaubriand beef, sliced
   1/8-inch thick by 1-inch wide by
   2-inches long
3 tablespoons oyster sauce
1/2 teaspoon curry powder
1 teaspoon sugar or honey
Pepper
2 cloves garlic, finely minced or
   pressed*

*1-1/2 tablespoons oil.
1 cup finely chopped, roasted peanuts
Grape leaves, blanched until pliable
   (soak 30 minutes if using jarred
   variety in several changes of water)
Optional: 1/2 cup very thinly sliced
   pork fat*

Marinate the first seven ingredients for 4 to 12 hours. Render very thin slices of pork fat, 1/2-inch wide and 2 inches long, in microwave until lightly translucent. Lay underside of grape leaf facing you and place marinated beef strip in middle, topped by pork fat, and scatter with peanuts. Roll up "burrito" style, brush with oil, place on hinged wire rack and grill. Serve with Nuoc Cham dipping sauce and rice noodles.

Serves 6.

Nuoc Cham Dipping Sauce

*4 tablespoons fish sauce
1 tablespoon white rice vinegar
1 tablespoon water
1-1/2 teaspoons sugar*

*Juice and pulp of one lime
1 clove garlic, minced
Thin slivers of jalapeños, about
   2 medium peppers*

Mix and adjust sweet, sour, hot balance to your liking.

Serve with Murphy-Good "Liar's Dice" Zinfandel or Merlot.

Murphy-Goode Estate Winery

Herb B.B.Q. Beef Marinade

3- to 5-pound beef tri tip
1/2 cup fresh rosemary
1/4 cup fresh sage
Pinch of thyme and oregano

2 cloves fresh garlic
1/2 tablespoon salt
1/2 teaspoon pepper
Olive oil

Process herbs in processor or blender. Rub surface of meat with olive oil and cover entire roast with herb mixture. Also, cut 3 or 4 pockets into roast and put some of the herb mixture in the pockets. Cover, or seal in plastic bag. Let stand several hours, or overnight in refrigerator. When ready to B.B.Q., remove roast from refrigerator and let stand 1 hour before cooking. B.B.Q. over hot coals until done to your liking.

Serves 4.

Recipe by Ed Seghesio.

Serve with Seghesio Barbera.

Seghesio Family Vineyards

Filet Mignon in a Creamy Peppercorn Sauce

4 to 6 filet mignon steaks, 1-inch thick *1 tablespoon olive oil*
1 tablespoon butter or margarine *6 tablespoons Brandy*

Remove all fat. In a wide frying pan over medium-high heat, melt butter with olive oil. Add meat, cook uncovered until browned on both sides (allow 3 to 5 minutes a side for rare). Keeping meat in the pan, add Brandy set aflame, shaking pan until flame dies or, if not, put a lid on it. Set filets aside, cover to keep warm while preparing the sauce.

Creamy Peppercorn Sauce

1/2 cup minced shallots *1/2 teaspoon tarragon leaves*
3/4 cup whipping cream *1 to 2 tablespoons green peppercorns*
1 tablespoon Dijon mustard *2 tablespoons White Oak Merlot*

To the same frying pan, add shallots, cook 2 to 3 minutes or until softened. Green peppercorns are purchased in brine or vinegar, rinse in cold water and drain. Add peppercorns, whipping cream, Dijon mustard, tarragon leaves and White Oak Merlot. Boil at high heat 3 to 4 minutes until thickened and shiny bubbles occur. Salt meat and pour sauce over filets. Serve with oven-roasted red potatoes with bell peppers.

Serves 4 to 6.

Serve with White Oak Merlot.

White Oak Vineyards and Winery

The Best Carrot Cake

2 cups flour, sifted
2 teaspoons cinnamon
2 teaspoons soda
1/2 teaspoon salt
3 eggs*
3/4 cup (saffola) oil*
3/4 cup buttermilk*

2 cups sugar
2 teaspoons vanilla
2 cups carrots, grated
1 (10-ounce) can pineapple, crushed
1 cup flaked coconut
1 cup nuts, chopped

Preheat oven to 350 degrees. In a large bowl, mix flour, soda, cinnamon, and salt. In another bowl, beat room temperature eggs. Add oil, buttermilk, sugar, and vanilla. Add to dry ingredients. In a separate bowl, mix carrots, pineapple, coconut, and nuts. Add to the above ingredients. Bake in a Pyrex dish for 55 minutes.

*At room temperature.

Carrot Cake Frosting

8 ounces cream cheese
1/2 cup butter
1 teaspoon vanilla

2 cups powdered sugar
1 teaspoon orange juice
1 teaspoon grated orange peel

Cream butter and cheese until fluffy. Add vanilla, sugar, orange juice, and orange peel. Mix until smooth. Frost cake and refrigerate until set.

Serves 8 to 10.

From Julio and Aileen Gallo family recipes.

Serve with Gallo of Sonoma 1998 Anapamu Late Harvest Riesling.

Gallo of Sonoma

Brandy Cake

1-1/2 cups raisins
1/2 cube butter
3/4 cup sugar
1 egg
1-1/2 cups flour
1 tablespoon powdered chocolate
  (Ghiradelli)
1/2 teaspoon each nutmeg, cloves and
  cinnamon
1/2 cup raisin juice (add enough
  Brandy if necessary to make the
  1/2 cup)

1 teaspoon baking soda (add this to
  the raisin juice)
4 tablespoons Brandy
1 cup chopped nuts

Frosting:
1 cube softened butter
2 cups powdered sugar
1 egg
4 tablespoons Brandy

Preheat oven to 350 degrees. Cover raisins with cold water. Bring to a boil and simmer 7 to 10 minutes. Cool thoroughly and drain raisins.

Cream sugar and butter; add egg. Sift flour with spices and chocolate, add to butter/sugar mixture, alternating with raisin juice. Add 4 tablespoons Brandy and mix well. Add nuts and raisins. Pour into two 8-inch, waxed paper-lined pans (greased and floured).

Bake at 350 degrees for 30 to 40 minutes; cool. Prepare frosting. In a mixing bowl, combine softened butter with 2 cups of sugar. Cream well. Add 1 egg and add 4 tablespoons of Brandy. Mix well. Frost cake.

Serves 8 to 10.

This cake recipe was given to me by a friend more than 30 years ago. She said it had been all over the South Pacific, where she had traveled. My children don't like fruit cake, but this is close and they love it. It travels well and is easy to make. The best part is you should make it a day or two ahead so it won't be too crumbly. Hope you like it!

Nancy Dalziel
Ellis Ranch

Summer Recipes

Smoked Salmon Canapés

1 cup sour cream
1/4 teaspoon finely grated lemon zest
1 loaf baguette, cut into 3/8-inch-
*   thick slices*

4 tablespoons unsalted butter, melted
1/2 pound sliced smoked salmon, cut
*   into 1/4-inch thick strips*
2 scallions, thinly sliced on the
*   diagonal*

In a small bowl, combine the sour cream and lemon zest. Transfer to a strainer lined with a paper coffee filter and set over a bowl. Let drain in the refrigerator until the sour cream is stiff, about 2 hours. Transfer lemon cream to a small bowl.

Meanwhile, preheat the oven to 350 degrees. Lightly brush both sides of the baguette slices with melted butter. Place on baking sheets and bake for about 5 minutes on both sides. Let cool completely. To assemble the canapés, spoon 1/4 teaspoon of the lemon cream in the center of each toast. Mound a salmon strip and garnish with the scallions. Arrange the canapés on a platter.

Makes 6 dozen canapés.

Serve with White Oak Chardonnay.

White Oak Vineyards and Winery

Simoneau Vineyards Cucumber Rounds
Topped with Chicken Salad

3 to 4 cucumbers
1 cup diced cooked white chicken meat
  (1 whole boneless breast)
2 teaspoons chopped fresh tarragon
1/4 cup mayonnaise

1/4 cup crème frâiche or sour cream
1/4 cup finely diced celery
1/4 cup chopped pecans
Salt and pepper to taste

Slice cucumbers 1/4-inch thick, put aside. Combine chicken and other ingredients in a bowl. Mix well. Spoon chicken salad onto cucumber slices and serve.

Makes about 36 appetizers.

Serve with Canyon Road Sauvignon Blanc.

Simoneau Vineyards

Chilled Sonoma Tomato-Vegetable Soup

16 *ripe tomatoes, blanched, peeled and seeded*
4 *English cucumbers, peeled and seeded*
4 *red bell peppers, peeled and seeded*
2 *celery stalks*
1/2 *medium onion, peeled*
1 *jalapeño pepper, cored, seeded and chopped fine*

1 *serrano chili, cored, seeded and chopped fine*
2 *ounces Sherry wine vinegar*
8 *ounces tomato juice*
3 *ounces olive oil*
Salt and freshly ground pepper
Cayenne pepper to taste
1/4 *cup chopped mixed herbs (Italian parsley, chives, cilantro, and tarragon)*

After vegetables have been peeled, cored, and seeded, cut everything into 1-inch pieces. Place them in a stainless steel bowl along with the jalapeño pepper and serrano chili. Add the vinegar, tomato juice, and olive oil. Season lightly with salt, freshly ground pepper, and cayenne pepper. Cover tightly and refrigerate overnight, stirring occasionally.

Place mixture in a food processor and, using the pulse setting, mince until the vegetables are fine but still have some texture to them. Return mixture to bowl and add the freshly chopped herbs. Correct the seasoning to taste. Chill well and serve in icy cold bowls.

Serves 12.

Recipe by Martin W. Courtman, Executive Chef, Chateau Souverain.

Serve with Chateau Souverain Zinfandel Blanc.

Chateau Souverain

Grits Casserole

1 cup grits
1 pound Cheddar cheese, grated
1/2 cup butter
1/4 teaspoon cayenne pepper
2 to 3 cloves garlic, minced

1/2 cup chopped jalapeño pepper
  (1 to 2 small cans)
1 cup hot grits
6 eggs, beaten

Cook grits according to package directions in water or chicken broth. Stir in cheese, butter, garlic, and jalapeños. Add eggs; stir and mix well. Pour into buttered casserole dish. Bake at 375 degrees for 35 to 40 minutes. Serve with BBQ tri-tip and a green salad.

Serves 6.

Serve with a Merlot.

Nancy Dalziel
Ellis Ranch

Butternut Squash Soup

6 tablespoons onion, chopped
4 tablespoons margarine
2 pounds (8 cups) butternut squash,
  cubed
3 cups water

4 chicken bouillon cubes
1/4 teaspoon ground black pepper
8 ounces cream cheese
Garlic to taste

Sauté onion in margarine. Add squash, water, bouillon, and black pepper. Bring to boil; cook 20 minutes, or until squash is tender. Purée in blender, adding cream cheese until smooth. Return to pan and heat through. Do not allow to boil.

Serves 6 to 8.

Joyce Fanucchi
Fanucchi Ranch

Tomato Pie

1 (9-inch) prepared pastry shell (the
   deeper the better)
5 to 6 medium tomatoes, coarsely
   chopped
1/2 cup mayonnaise
1/2 cup grated Parmesan cheese

1/4 teaspoon pepper
2 to 3 full sprigs basil, chopped
2 cloves garlic, minced
6 saltine crackers, crushed
2 tablespoons butter

Bake pastry shell according to directions.

Cut tomatoes in half horizontally to more easily remove seeds. Don't make a big deal out of this. Just hold a tomato half in your hand and thump once or twice on the side of your sink. Most of the seeds will fall out. Cut tomatoes in chunks and drain on paper towel.

Heap tomatoes in baked pie shell full to the top! Mix mayonnaise, garlic, cheese, pepper, and basil. Spread over top of tomatoes. Sprinkle with cracker crumbs and dot with butter. Bake at 425 degrees for 25 minutes. Let stand 10 to 15 minutes before cutting.

Serves 6 to 8.

This recipe has never failed to get rave reviews and is a great way to use all those tomatoes that come in at once in the garden! Throw a steak on the Barbie and open a bottle of 1996 Chateau Souverain Stuhlmuller Vineyards Cabernet. It won't get any better than this!!

Stuhlmuller Vineyards

Thai Grilled Chicken

16 boneless chicken thighs
8 stalks of lemon grass, cleaned and
*   coarsely chopped*
12 green onions, coarsely chopped
1/2 cup Thai fish sauce
2/3 cup sugar

1/2 cup raw peanuts, deep fried and
*   coarsely chopped*
3 tablespoons sugar
1 teaspoon salt
8 green onions, thinly sliced

Make the marinade by adding lemon grass (use only bottom third) and green onion to food processor and finely chop. Add fish sauce and sugar.

Stir to dissolve. Marinate thighs for at least three hours in this prepared marinade.

Grill over your favorite hardwood fire until done. Garnish with thinly sliced green onions and peanuts that have been tossed with the sugar and salt.

Serves 8 as an entrée.

Adapted from a recipe by Vorachoon Uchinda and Narin Cotipanang of Lemongrass Restaurant in Bangkok by Mary Lannin, Murphy-Goode Estate Winery.

Serve with Murphy-Goode Gewürztraminer or Fumé Blanc.

Murphy-Goode Estate Winery

Grilled Vegetable Salad with Greens, Tomatoes, Herbs, Olives and Cheese

3/4 cup Hanna olive oil
1/4 cup balsamic vinegar
1 large red onion, cut into 3/4-inch thick rounds
12 baby beets, stems trimmed to 1 inch, peeled and halved lengthwise
3 zucchini, each cut lengthwise into 4 slices
3 Japanese eggplants, each cut lengthwise into 4 slices
2 large red bell peppers, cut into 1-inch-wide strips

6 slices country-style French bread
10 cups mixed baby greens
4 large tomatoes, sliced
3 tablespoons chopped fresh basil
2 tablespoons chopped fresh chives or green onions
1 tablespoon chopped fresh marjoram
3/4 cup chilled soft goat cheese, crumbled (about 3 ounces)
1/2 cup freshly grated Pecorino Romano cheese (about 2 ounces)
3/4 cup brine-cured Kalamata olives

Prepare barbecue. Whisk 3/4 cup Hanna olive oil and vinegar in medium bowl to blend. Place onion, beets, zucchini, eggplants, and red bell peppers on baking sheet. Brush both sides with some of the vinaigrette. Sprinkle vegetables with salt and pepper. Grill vegetables until just cooked through, about 10 minutes per side for beets, 6 minutes per side for onion and 4 minutes per side for zucchini, eggplant, and peppers. (Vegetables may be grilled 1 hour ahead. Let stand at room temperature.) Brush bread with additional olive oil, sprinkle with pepper and grill bread until beginning to brown, about 2 minutes per side.

Arrange greens on a large platter. Overlap the tomatoes atop greens in center of platter. Sprinkle tomatoes with salt and pepper. Arrange grilled vegetables atop greens around the edge of the platter. Sprinkle tomatoes and vegetables with herbs and dot with the crumbled goat cheese. Sprinkle Romano cheese over all. Garnish with olives. Serve with the grilled bread in a basket.

Serves 6.

Serve with Hanna Sonoma Valley Hillside Blend.

Hanna Winery

Johnson's Famous Tri-Tip Sandwiches

10 pounds tri-tips
2 bottles red wine
2 cups oil
3 tablespoons Italian seasonings
40 small dinner rolls (any kind you like)

1 pint sour cream
1 jar prepared horseradish (fresh is best, of course)
A BBQ, and, of course, a good BBQer

Forty-eight hours prior to use, marinate the tri-tips in one part oil and two parts red wine. Sprinkle with Italian seasonings.

Slice the rolls in half and prepare the sauce. To do this, mix the sour cream with the horseradish and blend to your liking. We usually make several different levels of the sauce: (1) mostly sour cream and a little horseradish; (2) about half and half; and (3) more horseradish than sour cream.

BBQ the tri-tips to your liking and slice into thin slices. Serve on the rolls with a generous helping of your sauce of choice.

Makes 40 sandwiches.

Serve with Johnson's Alexander Valley Pinot Noir.

Johnson's Alexander Valley Wines

Mary's Barbecued Spareribs

1/2 cup olive oil
1/2 cup Zinfandel
1/3 cup tomato paste
2 teaspoons dried oregano
1 bay leaf, crumbled
2 large cloves garlic, minced

1 tablespoon brown sugar
1/2 to 1 teaspoon Tabasco sauce
1 teaspoon paprika
1 teaspoon salt
4 to 5 pounds pork spareribs

Whisk all sauce ingredients together in a very large bowl. Strip the tough membrane off the back of the ribs; hold a fork upright with the tines facing you. Rake the fork toward the meatier side of the rack, moving parallel to the bones. Cut the ribs apart, or in 2- to 4-rib sections, whichever you prefer. Toss well with the sauce, cover and refrigerate for 2 to 24 hours. Preheat oven to 350 degrees. Lay the ribs on racks placed over a pan filled with 1/2 inch of water. Roast for 1-1/2 to 2 hours. Or, if you prefer, you can roast them for 1 hour and transfer to a grill for the final cooking.

Serves 4 to 6.

© Mary Evely, Executive Chef, Simi Winery

Serve with Simi Zinfandel or Rosé.

Zinfandel and barbecue are the standard partners in California. It stands to reason, as Zinfandel has the fruit to match that of the tomato-based sauces and the acid to stand up to a little bit of heat. Bump up the brown sugar and Tabasco and you move this dish to a fruity blush wine that can handle the higher levels of sweet and hot.

Simi Winery

Caponata in Cucumber Cups

6 tablespoons olive oil
1 onion, chopped fine
1 clove garlic, minced
1 pound eggplant, chopped fine
3 red and/or yellow peppers, seeded and chopped fine
3 ribs celery, chopped fine
1 small (8 ounce) can tomato sauce
Salt and freshly ground pepper

2 tablespoons fresh oregano, chopped
2 tablespoons capers, rinsed and drained
3 anchovy fillets, chopped fine
1/2 cup Kalamata olives, pitted and cut into quarters
3 or 4 firm cucumbers
Fresh oregano leaves for garnish (optional)

Heat the oil in a large saucepan, add the onion and garlic and sauté until translucent. Add the eggplant and peppers and cook over medium heat for 10 minutes. Add tomato sauce, salt, pepper, and oregano, and cook until vegetables are tender but not mushy. Add the capers, anchovies, and olives and mix well. Remove from the heat and let stand at room temperature for 1 to 3 hours to develop flavors.

Peel cucumbers if the skins are waxed and cut into 1/2-inch slices. Make a well in the center of each slice with a small melon baller. Salt and drain slices on paper towels. Place a small spoonful of the caponata in the center of each cucumber slice. Garnish with a fresh oregano leaf (optional) and serve.

Note: For main course, serve at room temperature with chicken breasts seasoned with salt, pepper, oregano, and olive oil, and grilled or broiled.

Serves 15 to 20 as hors d'oeuvre,
or 6 as a side dish.

© Mary Evely, Executive Chef, Simi Winery

Serve with Simi Sauvignon Blanc or Pinot Noir.

Simi Winery

Grilled Lamb Burgers

1 pound lean ground lamb
2 tablespoons coarsely grated onion
2 tablespoons coarsely chopped parsley
1/2 teaspoon finely grated lemon zest
2 teaspoons White Oak Zinfandel
1/2 cup bread crumbs
Salt and pepper

1 small ripe avocado, peeled and pitted
2 teaspoons fresh lime juice
2 tablespoons plain yogurt
4 whole grain rolls
1 large ripe tomato, cut into 4 thick
  slices
1/2 cup alfalfa sprouts

In a bowl, lightly mix the lamb with the onion, parsley, lemon zest, bread crumbs, White Oak Zinfandel, salt and pepper. Form into 4 patties, each 3 inches across and 1 inch thick.

In a separate bowl, mash the avocado with the lime juice and yogurt. Season with salt and pepper to taste.

Grill the patties about 20 minutes, or until cooked through. Lightly toast the rolls. Place a lamb burger on each roll and top with the avocado mixture, tomato slices and alfalfa sprouts. Serve immediately.

Serves 4.

Serve with White Oak Zinfandel.

White Oak Vineyards and Winery

Pepperoni and Onion Pita Pizzas

2 (28-ounce) cans Italian tomatoes,
  peeled and drained
8 (8-inch) pita breads
1 tablespoon olive oil
1 medium red onion, sliced very thin
4 ounces pepperoni, sliced thin

3 cups grated Mozzarella cheese,
  (approx. 1/2 pound)
1 cup dry goat cheese
1/2 cup freshly grated Parmesan
  cheese
Crushed red pepper

Pinch the stem ends off the tomatoes and discard. Break the tomatoes into medium-sized pieces with your fingers. Put the tomatoes in a colander and drain.

Preheat oven to 475 degrees. Place 4 pitas on a large baking sheet. Brush the outer edges with olive oil. Spread each pita with one-eighth of each ingredient, except red pepper. Bake about 12 minutes, or until cheese begins to brown. Remove from oven and allow to set 2 to 3 minutes. Repeat with the other 4 pitas for second helpings.

Serves 4.

Serve with Field Stone Sangiovese.

Field Stone Winery

Caramelized Onions and Cambazola Pizza

Pizza Dough:

1-3/4 teaspoons yeast   *3-3/4 cups flour*
Pinch sugar   *1-1/2 teaspoons salt*
1-1/3 cups warm water   *Cornmeal*
1/4 cup olive oil

Dissolve sugar and yeast in the water. Let stand for about 5 to 10 minutes until the yeast mixture is foamy. Add 1 cup of the flour and stir until well blended. Add salt and olive oil and mix well. Blend in the balance of the flour one cup at a time. Knead on a lightly floured counter until the dough is no longer sticky. Place in an oiled bowl and cover with plastic wrap. Let rise in a warm place until dough has doubled in volume, one to two hours. Place a pizza stone (if you have one) in the oven at least 30 minutes prior to cooking and preheat oven to 450 degrees F. Divide dough in two. Roll each out on a well floured counter. Slide onto a pizza paddle or cookie sheet previously sprinkled with cornmeal.

Topping:

Extra virgin olive oil   *20 pitted and quartered Kalamata*
4 yellow onions, finely chopped   *olives*
1 cup grated Mozzarella cheese   *Fresh ground black pepper*
3/4 cup crumbled Cambazola cheese

Sauté onions over very low heat for 20 to 30 minutes, stirring often, until the onions are lightly browned and caramelized. Drizzle olive oil on the dough. Sprinkle with grated Mozzarella. Cover with caramelized onions. Dot with crumbled Cambazola. Top with olives and fresh ground pepper. Bake on the preheated stone until crust is golden brown.

Makes two large pizzas.

Serve with Hafner Cabernet Sauvignon.

Hafner Vineyard

Poached Salmon with Strawberry Salsa

Court Bouillon for Poaching Fish:

6 cups water
2 cups dry white wine
1/2 cup white wine vinegar
1 lemon, cut into quarters
1 bay leaf
1 carrot, chopped
2 yellow onions, quartered

2 tablespoons kosher salt
1 medium leek, white and green parts,
  chopped
3 sprigs of Italian parsley
1 bay leaf
2 tablespoons kosher salt

Combine all of the ingredients in a stockpot and bring to a boil over high heat.

Reduce the heat and simmer, uncovered, for 20 to 30 minutes, skimming off any foam that forms on the surface.

Makes about 8 cups.

Strawberry Salsa:

1 pint strawberries, stemmed and diced
Black pepper in a mill
1 to 2 serrano chiles, minced
1/2 red onion, minced
3 tablespoons strawberry, raspberry,
  or red wine vinegar

2 tablespoons minced cilantro
Kosher salt
Black pepper in a mill

Place the strawberries and the sugar in a medium bowl and toss lightly. Cover and refrigerate for at least 1 hour. Remove the bowl from the refrigerator. Add the serrano chiles, onion, vinegar, and cilantro, and toss together lightly. Season with salt and pepper. Let the salsa rest at room temperature for at least 20 minutes before serving. Store, covered, in the refrigerator for up to 2 days.

Makes about 2 cups.

Preparing Salmon:

*8 cups Court Bouillon, at room
  temperature*

1 cup Strawberry Salsa

*4 to 6 salmon steaks or fillets, 6 to 8
  ounces each*

Pour the court bouillon into a large nonreactive pan or fish poacher. Add the salmon in a single layer and set the pan, uncovered, over medium-low heat. Using an instant-read thermometer, allow the temperature of the liquid to rise slowly to about 160 degrees F. Maintain the temperature for 10 minutes, adjusting the heat if necessary.

Remove the pan from the heat, cover it, and let the salmon rest for 20 minutes. Allowing fish to cool to room temperature in the poaching liquid results in very tender fish. Using a slotted spoon, transfer the salmon to individual plates. Top each portion with a generous spoonful of salsa and serve immediately, with the remaining salsa on the side.

Serves 4 to 6.

Recipe from © Michele Anna Jordan, from California Home Cooking (Harvard Common Press, 1997).

Serve with 1999 Clos du Bois Alexander Valley Reserve Chardonnay.

Clos du Bois Winery

Savory Mushroom Quiche

1/2 pound mushrooms, chopped
3 tablespoons butter
1/2 cup saltines (about 14 crackers),
  crushed
1 bunch green onions, chopped,
  including tender green part of tops

2 tablespoons butter
8 ounces Jack cheese, grated
1 cup cottage cheese
3 eggs
1/4 teaspoon red pepper
1/4 teaspoon paprika

Sauté chopped mushrooms in 3 tablespoons butter until soft. Crush crackers and add to mushrooms. Mix well. Press against bottom and sides of baking dish to form crust. Cool.

Sauté onions in 2 tablespoons butter. Spread mixture over crust of mushrooms and crackers. Sprinkle grated cheese over that.

Blend cottage cheese, eggs, and seasonings. Pour into mushroom-onion crust. Bake at 350 degrees for 20 minutes (or 400 degrees for 5 to 10 minutes). Let stand at room temperature for 15 minutes before serving.

Serves 8.

Vail Vista Vineyards

Penne with Peas and Prosciutto

2 cups veal stock
1-1/2 pounds fresh green peas
1/2 pound prosciutto, very thinly sliced
1 small onion, peeled and minced
1 garlic clove, peeled and crushed
2 small, hot chili peppers
1/4 cup olive oil

2 tablespoons chopped mixed fresh herbs: thyme, parsley or sage
1/4 teaspoon freshly ground white pepper
Salt
1 pound penne pasta
Freshly grated Pecorino Romano or Parmesan cheese

Bring the veal stock to a boil; turn the heat low and let reduce slowly until only 4 to 5 tablespoons of stock remain.

Shell the peas and put to one side. Cut the prosciutto in small squares. Cut chili peppers in half lengthwise, remove the seeds, core, and mince.

Heat the olive oil in a suitably large frying pan and sauté the onions and garlic until translucent. Add the prosciutto and fry briefly over high heat, stirring constantly. Add the peas, herbs, and chili peppers, and pour in the reduced veal stock. Season with pepper and, if necessary, salt. Simmer a few minutes, stirring occasionally.

In the meantime, cook the penne in boiling salted water until al dente. Drain and mix immediately with the peas and prosciutto mixture. Transfer to 4 pre-warmed plates and sprinkle with grated cheese.

Serves 4.

Recipe by Don Bodio, Trentadue Winery.

Serve with Trentadue 1998 Carignane Rosé.

Trentadue Winery

Pulled Pork Sandwich

8 to 10 pounds pork shoulder picnic roast
Your favorite barbecue sauce

Coleslaw (recipe follows)
10 to 12 soft French bread buns

The secret for "real barbecue" is to keep the cooking chamber temperature in the 210- to 250-degree range throughout the cooking period and to cook the meat for a long time. A pork shoulder picnic roast should cook for 10 hours.

There is a meat and a skin side to the picnic roast. Liberally salt and pepper the meat side of the picnic. Allow the meat to reach room temperature. Light one side of your gas grill and preheat the cooking chamber to 250 degrees. Place the picnic on the opposite side of the lit cooking chamber and add two chunks of hickory over the lit side of the grill. Wrap the hickory in heavy duty foil and poke some holes in the foil to let the smoke out.

Hold the temperature at 250 degrees for six hours, adding two more hickory chunks every half-hour or so, depending on how soon the grill stops smoking. At the sixth hour, flip the picnic skin side down and lower the heat to 215 degrees for 4 more hours. Continue to add hickory chunks as before. After 10 hours' cooking, remove the picnic and let cool for 1/2 hour.

Pull off the skin. If there is excess fat on the meat, gently scrape off with a knife. Grasp the bone and give it a twist and it should pull right out with little resistance. Chop the meat into a medium dice and mix the brown outer meat with the white inner meat. Make your sandwich, piling as much meat as a soft bun will hold and giving a squirt of your favorite barbecue sauce and a dollop of coleslaw.

Serves 10.

Coleslaw

2 garlic cloves, minced
1 teaspoon salt
2 cups light cream
1 cup sugar

1 cup apple cider vinegar
4 tablespoons mayonnaise
1 head cabbage
2 to 3 carrots, grated

Make a paste by covering the minced garlic with salt on a cutting board and mashing the garlic, in a rocking motion, with the side of a knife blade. Place all ingredients, except carrots and cabbage, in a lidded jar and shake well to make a dressing.

Look for a tight head of green cabbage. Core and slice the cabbage very thin. Grate the carrots. Place cabbage and carrots in a bowl, pour dressing over. Toss well and refrigerate overnight.

Serves 10.

Carole and Mike Farrell
Fox Hill Vineyard

Grilled Eggplant Parmesan

2 eggplants, 1 pound each
1/3 cup olive oil
1 tablespoon dried Italian herb mix
* or dried oregano*
2 tablespoons chopped fresh basil

10 to 12 ounces Mozzarella cheese
Sliced fresh tomatoes
1/3 cup grated Parmesan cheese
3 tablespoons chopped parsley
Salt and pepper

Rinse eggplant, cut each crosswise into 3/4-inch rounds, and discard stems and smooth ends. Lay slices side-by-side on a large tray or 2 or 3 baking sheets, about 12 by 15 inches. In a small bowl, mix oil, Italian herb mix, and fresh basil. Brush cut sides of eggplant with oil mixture. Cut Mozzarella cheese and tomatoes into thin slices, making 1 piece for each eggplant round.

Set eggplant rounds on a grill over a solid bed of medium-hot coals or medium-high heat on gas barbeque. Close lid of barbeque. Cook until eggplant is very soft when pressed, creamy inside (cut to test), and browned, 6 to 8 minutes; turn once. Place rounds in pan. Top each eggplant round with a slice of Mozzarella cheese and tomato. Cook over barbeque until cheese and tomato soften. Sprinkle with Parmesan cheese and parsley. Season to taste with salt and pepper. Serve with a chilled green salad.

Serves 4.

Serve with Sausal Zinfandel.

Sausal Winery

Cornish Game Hens Madeira

3 Cornish game hens, cut in halves
5 tablespoons melted butter
1/4 cup Dijon mustard
2 tablespoons fresh rosemary
2 cloves garlic, minced
1/2 shallot, minced

1/2 bottle of Madeira
4 tablespoons butter
1/4 cup Dijon mustard
Rosemary

Heat oven to 450 degrees. Mix butter, mustard, rosemary, shallot, and garlic. Salt and pepper the hens. Coat the hens with mustard mixture. Place in roasting pan. Roast at 450 degrees for approximately 30 minutes.

Remove hens. Degrease pan, if necessary. Add Madeira to pan with 4 tablespoons butter, 1/4 cup Dijon mustard and rosemary. Heat, letting alcohol burn off. Heat and drizzle sauce over hens before serving. Best when served with green beans also topped with leftover sauce.

Serves 6.

Serve with Geyser Peak Viognier.

Geyser Peak Winery

Spicy Brunch Casserole

8 thick slices French bread
2 cups shredded Cheddar cheese
2 cups shredded Sonoma Jack cheese
2 large chiles, roasted
1 pound sausage, cooked and
  crumbled

8 eggs
2 cups milk
2 teaspoons salt
1/2 teaspoon pepper
1/4 teaspoon garlic powder

Butter bread and place buttered side down in a 9 x 13-inch casserole dish. Sprinkle chiles and sausage over bread. Beat eggs together with milk and seasonings. Pour over other ingredients. Top with shredded cheeses. Cover dish with foil and bake in a preheated oven at 325 degrees for about 50 minutes.

Brown cheese under broiler, uncovered. This recipe may be made one day ahead and stored in the refrigerator. Serve with fresh fruit.

Serves 6.

Serve with White Oak Zinfandel or Chateau Souverain Reserve Zinfandel.

Chalk's Bend Vineyard

Lamb Sosaties with Fruit

1-1/2 cups cider vinegar
3 tablespoons apricot or pineapple jam
1-1/2 tablespoons <u>each</u> curry powder,
  salt and brown sugar (firmly packed)
1/4 teaspoon pepper
4 small, dried hot chile peppers,
  crushed (use only 1 or 2 for a milder
  marinade)

2 medium onions, sliced
3 garlic cloves, mashed
6 fresh lemon or orange leaves, or 2
  dried bay leaves
4 pounds lean boneless lamb, cubed
About 6 cups fruit: pitted apricots,
  pineapple chunks, cantaloupe
  wedges and spiced crabapples

In a pan, combine vinegar, jam, curry powder, salt, brown sugar, pepper, chile peppers, onions, garlic, and lemon, orange or bay leaves. Bring to boil to blend the flavors; cool. Pour marinade over meat, cover and refrigerate 8 to 10 hours, or overnight. Just before barbequing the meat, remove from marinade and string on skewers. Place meat over medium-hot coals, turning grill to brown on all sides, a total of 15 to 20 minutes.

Strain the marinade, discarding onions and leaves. Bring liquid to a boil and simmer about 5 minutes to concentrate it. Baste meat occasionally with marinade.

String fruit on skewers and lay on top of meat during last 5 to 10 minutes of cooking. Baste the fruit and meat with marinade. The fruit will also help baste the meat and should be on the grill long enough to be thoroughly heated but not soft.

Serves 8.

Serve with deLorimier "Mosaic" Red Meritage.

deLorimier Winery

Italian Sausage-Stuffed Mushrooms
with Seghesio Zinfandel

18 to 20 large mushrooms
1/2 pound Italian sausage (hot or mild)
1/2 cup chopped onion
3 to 6 cloves fresh garlic, minced
3 to 4 tablespoons olive oil

1/4 to 1/3 cup Seghesio Zinfandel
1/4 cup Italian seasoned bread crumbs
1 egg
1/4 cup freshly grated Parmesan cheese

Preheat oven to 350 degrees. Remove stems from mushrooms. Chop stems. Brown the sausage, onion, garlic, and chopped stems in olive oil. Drain well. Add wine to drained mixture and simmer until liquid is slightly reduced. Remove from heat. Mix in bread crumbs, egg, and cheese.

Stuff mushrooms slightly over full. Bake at 350 degrees for 15 to 20 minutes. Sprinkle with extra Parmesan cheese before serving.

Makes appetizers for 4 to 6.

From the kitchen of Ed Seghesio.

Serve with Seghesio Sonoma Zinfandel.

Seghesio Family Vineyards

Chilled Mussels Topped with Mango Salsa

*1 pound Prince Edward Island
  mussels
1 cup Alexander Valley Vineyards
  1998 Chardonnay*

*1 bay leaf
1 lemon, juiced*

Start by placing wine, lemon juice and bay leaf in a large pot and bring to a boil. Place mussels in boiling liquid and cover; mussels will open after 2 minutes. Promptly remove after opening so as not to overcook. Place mussels in a clean bowl and chill.

Mango Salsa

*2 mangos, diced
1 jalapeno pepper, seeded and minced
1 clove garlic, finely chopped
2 tablespoons cilantro, chopped*

*1 tablespoon rice wine vinegar
3 tablespoons olive oil
1/2 small onion, finely chopped
Salt and pepper to taste*

Peel mango, then cut fruit away from seed. Place all ingredients in bowl and mix gently. For presentation, remove top half shell of mussel, detach mussel from bottom shell and top with mango salsa.

Serves 4 for hors d'oeuvres.

Serve with Alexander Valley Vineyards 1999 Chardonnay

Alexander Valley Vineyards

Momma's BBQ'd Spare Ribs

3 to 4 pounds meaty spare ribs, cut in pieces of 2 ribs each
2 lemons, sliced
1 large onion, sliced
1 cup catsup

1/3 cup Worcestershire sauce
1 teaspoon chili powder
1 teaspoon salt
2 dashes Tabasco sauce
2 cups water

On each 2-rib piece of meat, place a slice of onion and a slice of lemon, anchored with a toothpick. Place in shallow pan for 30 minutes in a 400-degree oven while making the sauce.

To make sauce, put catsup, Worcestershire sauce, chile powder, salt, Tabasco, and water in a saucepan. Bring all ingredients to a boil and pour over ribs. Bake 1 hour, or until tender. Baste often (every 15 minutes). Add extra water if necessary.

Serves 6 to 8.

Serve with a Sausal Zinfandel.

Linda Lynch
Graperfection

Eggplant Salad with Fontina and Pesto

*2 medium eggplants (about 2-1/2
    pounds total)*
Salt and freshly ground pepper
Olive oil
*8 ounces Fontina cheese, cut into
    small pieces*
6 green onions, diagonally sliced
*1 large green pepper, seeded and
    diced*
*1 cup roasted sweet red pepper, cut
    in thin julienne strips*
Lettuce

Pesto dressing:
1 large clove garlic
1/2 cup firmly packed basil leaves
1/4 cup grated Parmesan cheese
2 tablespoons white wine vinegar
1/3 cup olive oil
Salt and freshly ground pepper

Slice, but do not peel, eggplant into 1/2-inch-thick rounds. Sprinkle both sides with salt and place rounds on paper towels for about 45 minutes. Meanwhile, combine garlic, basil, cheese, vinegar, and oil in a blender or food processor and whirl until smooth. Season to taste with salt and pepper. Cover and set aside. Pat any excess moisture from eggplant slices. Arrange in single layers on two large baking sheets. Preheat broiler. Lightly brush both sides of eggplant with olive oil. Place baking sheets 2 to 4 inches below broiler element and cook, turning slices once, until lightly browned. (You may need to do this in batches.) Remove, cool slightly, and cut into large pieces. Place in a bowl and add Fontina, onions, green pepper, red pepper, and dressing. Toss gently to combine, and serve on a bed of lettuce.

Serves 4 to 6.

From Julio and Aileen Gallo family recipes.

Serve with Gallo of Sonoma 1997 Laguna Vineyard Chardonnay

Gallo of Sonoma

Country Blackberry Cobbler

2 cups fresh or frozen blackberries　　*1 cup sugar*
1/2 cup sugar　　*2 teaspoons baking powder*
6 tablespoons butter　　*1/2 teaspoon salt*
3/4 cup flour　　*3/4 cup milk*

Place blackberries in a bowl with 1/2 cup sugar. Mix well and set aside. Preheat oven to 350 degrees. Melt butter in baking pan. Sift together flour, sugar, baking powder, and salt. Add milk. Mix well. Pour this batter into pan with melted butter (do not mix). Pour fruit over batter. Bake for 50 minutes.

Serves 6.

Wasson Vineyards

Cabernet Poached Pears

1/2 bottle Hanna Cabernet Sauvignon
1-1/2 cups water
1/2 to 3/4 cup sugar

1 sprig fresh basil or thyme
2 pounds firm ripe pears, such as
  Bartlett or Bosc

In a large, non-reactive saucepan, combine wine, water, sugar, and basil or thyme. Bring to a simmer. Meanwhile, leaving the stems intact, peel pears with a vegetable peeler and core them. Place pears in simmering syrup as you finish peeling them. Simmer until pears are cooked through but not mushy, 20 to 30 minutes.

Remove pears from syrup with a slotted spoon and reduce syrup to about three-quarters of its original volume. Let pears and syrup cool separately to room temperature, then combine and refrigerate until ready to serve.

Serves 6.

Serve with Hanna Alexander Valley Cabernet Sauvignon.

Hanna Winery

Carrie's Coconut Shortcakes

4-1/2 cups flour (dip and level cup)
1 cup sugar
3 teaspoons baking powder
1-1/2 teaspoons baking soda
1 teaspoon salt
12 tablespoons (3/4 cup) unsalted
  butter, chilled

1-1/3 cups buttermilk
2 egg yolks
1 teaspoon vanilla
2-1/3 cups shredded coconut (reserve
  1/3 cup for garnish)
1 egg white

Toast the coconut in a 400-degree oven on a baking sheet for 8 to 10 minutes, or until lightly toasted. Check and stir while toasting. Increase oven heat to 450 degrees.

In a large mixing bowl, combine the flour, sugar, baking powder, baking soda, and salt. Mix well. Cut the chilled butter into 1/2-inch slices and sprinkle over the dry mix. Cut the butter into the mix to form large pea-sized crumbs. (You may accomplish this in a food processor in several batches of dry mix and butter, pulsing until coarse crumbs are formed, or you can mix by hand.

Combine the buttermilk, egg yolks, and vanilla and stir together in a small mixing bowl. Set aside. Sprinkle the 2 cups toasted coconut over the crumb mixture and fold in with a rubber spatula. Pour the egg-buttermilk mixture over the crumb mixture and fold with a rubber spatula. You may then knead the mixture gently 8 to 10 times to combine the dry and wet ingredients together into an elastic shortcake dough. Don't over-knead. All you want to do is to make a dough that comes together.

Sprinkle a tablespoon or so of flour onto a board. Press the dough into a round, flat shape with your hands. Sprinkle a little flour on top, and, with a rolling pin, roll out from the center to form dough into a 3/4-inch thick, 15-1/2-inch x 10-inch rectangle. Cut with a 2-1/4-inch round or fluted round cutter (dip in flour to prevent sticking) and place "cakes" on a parchment-lined or ungreased baking sheet. Space at least 2 inches apart. You may gather scraps of dough together and gently press them together and re-roll to cut extra cakes.

Brush tops with 1 egg white mixed with 1 tablespoon water. Sprinkle with granulated sugar and coconut. Bake in preheated 450-degree oven for 5 minutes. <u>Don't open the door</u>. Turn oven down to 425 degrees for 8 more minutes, then check. Reverse the pan position and continue to bake another 2 to 3 minutes. Check to see that the cakes are lightly golden on top and that they are set (firm to the touch). Remove from oven and cool on rack. Serve with whipped cream and fresh berries.

Makes 18 cakes
(plus extras if you re-roll the scraps).

© *Jimtown Store 2000.*

Jimtown Store

Fall Recipes

Palmieres with Olive Tapenade

2 anchovy fillets, rinsed
1 cup Kalamata olives
1 tablespoon drained capers
1 garlic clove

1/4 cup olive oil
1 tablespoon Dijon mustard
Frozen sheet puff pastry dough,
  defrosted in refrigerator overnight

Place anchovies, olives, capers, garlic clove, olive oil, and mustard in a blender or food processor. Blend or grind to a paste consistency. If too thick, add a little more olive oil and blend a little longer.

Roll out a sheet of puff pastry to 1/8-inch thickness. Spread a fine layer of tapenade on dough. Roll the two long edges until they meet in the middle. Wrap in plastic wrap and refrigerate for at least an hour, or place in the freezer until just frozen. Repeat with second sheet.

Preheat oven to 400 degrees. Slice roll into 1/2-inch pieces and place on a parchment-lined baking sheet. Bake for 8 to 12 minutes, or until golden and puffed. Serve immediately.

Makes approximately 50 appetizers.

Serve with Geyser Peak's Shiraz Sparkling Wine.

Simoneau Vineyards

Zuppa d'Oro (Gold Soup)

2 pounds zucca or butternut squash, halved
1/4 cup olive oil
1 tablespoon fresh thyme, minced
1 tablespoon fresh rosemary, minced
1 tablespoon fresh oregano, minced
1 teaspoon black peppercorns, coarsely ground
6 garlic cloves, roasted

4 tablespoons butter
1/2 medium onion, minced
2 cups beef broth, canned
1/2 cup Madeira or Dry Sherry
1 cup milk or half-and-half
1 tablespoon chipotle in adobo sauce (available in Mexican food sections)

Cut squash in half and remove seeds. Mix olive oil with herbs and pepper. Rub cut surfaces of the squash with the oil and herbs. Place squash cut side down with 2 to 3 garlic cloves in the cavity. Bake at 350 degrees for 30 minutes, until fork pierces the flesh easily. Cool; remove flesh from the shell.

Purée squash with herbs and garlic. Melt butter, cook onion until translucent; add broth and squash, bring to a simmer, blending with a whisk. Remove from heat. Add Madeira or Sherry, milk and chipotle; whisk. Season with salt. Serve hot.

Serves 8.

Serve with Field Stone Sangiovese.

Field Stone Winery

Leek and Potato Soup
with Port and Gorgonzola

2 large bunches of leeks
1 to 2 onions, coarsely chopped
1 stick unsalted butter
1/2 cup Gallo Family Port
1 large can (46 ounces) chicken broth
4 cups water

4 large baking potatoes, peeled and
  diced
1/8 teaspoon cayenne pepper
3/4 cup heavy cream
1/4 pound Gorgonzola cheese
Salt and freshly ground pepper

Trim off the tough dark green parts of the leeks. Quarter the white part and tender green lengthwise and rinse well in a bowl of cold water. Leeks can be very sandy. Slice the leeks into large dice, put in a bowl and add fresh cold water to cover. With your hands, transfer the leeks to a colander. Measure the leeks. If there is less than 6 cups, add coarsely chopped onions to make up the difference. In a very large flameproof casserole, combine the butter and leeks. Cover and cook over low heat for 10 minutes, stirring once. Uncover and cook, stirring occasionally at first and then more frequently, until the leeks are golden brown, 25 to 30 minutes.

Add the Port to the casserole and scrape up the browned residue on the bottom of the pan. Add the chicken broth and the water. Bring to a boil. Add the potatoes and cayenne, reduce the heat to moderate and cook, partially covered, for 20 minutes. In a blender, purée the soup in batches until smooth. Return to the casserole. (The soup may be prepared ahead to this point, up to 2 days. Reheat before proceeding.) In blender, combine cream and cheese. Return soup to boil. Stir in cheese and season with salt and black pepper to taste.

Serves 8.

From Julio and Aileen Gallo family recipes.

Serve with 1997 Gallo of Sonoma Frei Ranch Zinfandel

Gallo of Sonoma

117

Risotto Milanese

1 medium onion, chopped	*4 ounces Trentadue Chardonnay*
1/2 tablespoon butter	*4 cups heated chicken stock*
1 tablespoon olive oil	*1/8 cup cream*
12 ounces Arborio rice	*1 cup Parmesan cheese, grated*
6 strands saffron	

In a medium-sized, heavy-bottomed saucepan, sauté the onion in butter and olive oil until golden, along with the saffron. Add the rice and stir until well coated and translucent. Add the Trentadue Chardonnay and cook until nearly evaporated. Stir in 1 cup of hot stock and simmer gently.

When the stock has been absorbed, add another cup and continue in this way throughout 18 to 20 minutes, or until most of the stock has been absorbed. Stir gently and infrequently so as not to smash the rice. Stir in the cream and cheese. Salt to taste. Remove from heat, cover and set aside for 2 minutes before serving.

The traditional way to eat Risotto Milanese is to serve it in a bowl and push the risotto up the side to the top edge and eat all the way around the bowl down toward the center. My father pours a little red wine, usually Sangiovese or Zinfandel, in the bowl with a little extra Parmesan, mixes it all up and the pushes it up along the sides of the bowl.

Serves 4.

Recipe contributed by Don Bodio, Trentadue Winery.

Serve with Trentadue 1996 Alexander Valley Sangiovese.

Trentadue Winery

Clams Linguini

6 to 8 ounces linguini pasta
1/2 cube butter
1 small onion, chopped
3 tablespoons chopped parsley
3 to 4 cloves garlic, minced

1 can baby clams
Fresh ground pepper to taste
Freshly grated Parmesan cheese to
taste (about 1/4 cup)

Sauté onion and garlic over low heat for 5 to 10 minutes. Add parsley, pepper, and broth from the clams.

Bring water to a boil and cook pasta according to package directions for al dente. Drain!

Add clams to onion-garlic mixture and toss with pasta and Parmesan cheese. Serve immediately. Pair with a garden-fresh salad and a baguette.

Serves 2.

Serve with Stuhlmuller Vineyards Chardonnay.

Stuhlmuller Vineyards

Grilled Dove Breast with Dates and Bacon

12 dove breasts	*12 strips bacon*
1/4 cup teriyaki sauce	*Wooden skewers*
12 large dried dates	

Marinate dove breasts in teriyaki sauce for 1 hour or overnight. Remove the pits from dates and flatten. Roll the dove breast in the flattened dates. Roll the bacon strip around the breast and dates. Skewer 3 rolled breasts on a wooden skewer. Grill over low heat until bacon is completely cooked and browned.

Serves 4.

Serve with Alexander Valley Merlot.

Del Rio Vineyard
Rio Vista

Tamale-Stuffed Peppers

1 tablespoon olive oil	*2 cups canned, chopped tomatoes*
1 pound ground beef	*1-1/2 teaspoon salt*
1/2 cup chopped onion	*1/2 cup yellow corn meal*
1 can small pitted black olives	*6 green peppers, core and seeds*
1 cup whole kernel corn, drained	*removed, parboiled*
3/4 cup grated cheese	

Brown beef and onion in pan with olive oil. Drain excess liquid. Add olives, corn, and cheese. Put aside. Cook 2 cups of tomatoes with salt and corn meal for 5 to 10 minutes. Add to meat mixture. Stuff peppers with meat-tomato mixture and sprinkle tops with 1/4 cup grated cheese. Bake in 350-degree oven for 1 hour.

Serves 6.

Wasson Vineyards

Chilean Sea Bass with Olive Tapenade and Saffron Cous Cous

*1 cup Kalamata olives, pitted and
  finely chopped*
*1 sprig rosemary, stemmed and
  chopped*
1 anchovy, minced
1 clove garlic, peeled and minced
2 tablespoons Hanna olive oil
Salt and pepper to taste
1/4 cup Hanna Chardonnay

Pinch saffron
2 cups chicken stock
1 (12-ounce) package cous cous
Salt and pepper to taste

4 6-ounce pieces Chilean sea bass
1 clove garlic, peeled and mashed
Salt and pepper to taste
Hanna olive oil for drizzling

For the tapenade, combine the olives, rosemary, anchovy, garlic, and olive oil in a small bowl. Season and set aside.

For the cous cous, combine the wine and saffron in a small bowl and set aside. In a medium saucepan over high heat, add the stock and bring to a boil. Remove from the heat, incorporate the cous cous and wine mixture, cover and set aside. When all the liquid is absorbed, fluff the cous cous with a fork.

Preheat the oven to 450 degrees. Place the sea bass on a baking sheet, rub with garlic, and season with salt and pepper. Drizzle with Hanna olive oil, place in the oven and bake for 15 minutes, or to desired doneness. Remove from the oven and set aside. Spoon some of the cous cous onto a plate. Place a piece of sea bass over the cous cous and spoon some of the tapenade on top.

Serves 4.

Serve with Hanna Russian River Valley Chardonnay.

Hanna Winery

Crab Cakes

1 cup clarified butter	*1 ear fresh corn, cut off cob*
1/3 cup green onions, thinly sliced	*2 tablespoons heavy cream*
1 pound crab meat	*1-1/2 teaspoon marjoram*
1 egg	*4 tablespoons red pepper*
3/4 cup bread crumbs	

Melt 2 tablespoons of the butter. Add green onions and remove from heat. Place crab meat in bowl, beat the egg and mix with crab. Add 1/2 cup bread crumbs, corn, cream, marjoram, pepper, and green onion. Mix by hand.

Form into 8 patties (3 inches by 1/2 inch). Roll patties lightly in remaining bread crumbs. Heat remaining butter in large sauté pan. Place crab cakes in pan (they should sizzle), cook at lowest setting for 5 to 6 minutes. Cakes should be golden, not brown. Serve with salsa.

Makes 8 patties.

Serve with Murphy-Goode Reserve Chardonnay - Island Block.

Murphy-Goode Estate Winery

Grilled Chicken Breast
with Black Bean and Roasted Corn Salsa

8 boneless, skinless chicken breast halves
1-1/2 cups dried black beans (soak overnight in water)
2 garlic cloves, chopped
4 ears of corn
1/2 cup red bell peppers, chopped finely
1 small jalapeño chili, seeded and chopped finely

1/4 cup red onion, chopped finely
1-1/2 tablespoons red wine vinegar
1/2 tablespoons balsamic vinegar
1/2 tablespoon fresh lime juice
1/2 teaspoon ground coriander
1 teaspoon oregano
1/4 cup Italian parsley, chopped
1/4 cup cilantro, chopped
6 ounces olive oil
Salt and freshly ground pepper

Marinate the chicken breast in 4 ounces of the olive oil and the stems of the fresh parsley and cilantro (which may be chopped slightly) for 8 hours. Remove husks from the corn and lightly coat with a little of the olive oil. Place on a baking sheet and roast at 350 degrees for about 40 minutes, or until kernels are golden brown. Cool at room temperature, then remove kernels, scraping the cobs and saving any liquid along with the kernels. Drain the beans and put into a saucepan with 1 teaspoon salt. Cover with water and cook over medium heat until tender. Drain. Put aside. Sweat the garlic and red onions in the remaining olive oil. Add the peppers and coriander and cook for 2 more minutes. Stir in the beans and corn, then add vinegars and lime juice. Heat to a simmer (if more liquid is needed to moisten the salsa, use chicken stock or water). Simmer for 5 minutes. Remove from heat and mix in the parsley, cilantro and oregano. Season with salt and freshly ground pepper. Take the chicken from the marinade, season with salt and freshly ground pepper. Grill both sides until done, about 3 to 4 minutes, depending on the size of the breasts. Serve salsa under the grilled chicken breasts and garnish with cilantro sprigs.

Serves 8.

Recipe by Martin W. Courtman, Executive Chef, Chateau Souverain.

Serve with Chateau Souverain Viognier.

Chateau Souverain

Sausage and Sweet Potato Salad
with Cider Mustard Vinaigrette

2-1/2 tablespoons grainy Dijon mustard
2 tablespoons maple syrup (sugar is
fine if you don't have real maple
syrup)
1/3 cup cider vinegar
1/3 cup balsamic vinegar
2 cups olive oil
1/2 teaspoon salt
1/4 teaspoon freshly ground black
pepper

6 pounds garnet (orange-fleshed)
sweet potatoes
4 tablespoons olive oil
2 teaspoons kosher salt
2 scallions, green and white parts
(sliced on the diagonal)
8 sausages of your choice (poultry
sausages are nice and lower in fat)

Combine first 7 ingredients to make vinaigrette dressing. Mix well and put aside. (Recipe will yield about 2-1/2 cups.)

Preheat oven to 475 degrees. Peel and cut the sweet potatoes into bite-sized cubes. Toss with olive oil and salt. Roast in a single layer until tender and browned, 30 to 45 minutes. Set aside. Brown sausages in a skillet with one tablespoon olive oil. Cut into bite-sized chinks. Toss the sweet potatoes, onions, and sausages, with amount of dressing you prefer. Taste for salt . Add black pepper to taste, if desired. Serve warm or at room temperature. May be made one day ahead and reheated.

Serves 15 to 20 for a picnic or buffet, or
8 for a main dish.

Extra dressing keeps a while and may be used on any hearty salad (such as bean or potato).

Jimtown Store

Roasted Pumpkin Risotto with Fresh Sage

8 miniature pumpkins
Salt and freshly ground white pepper
16 fresh sage leaves
3 tablespoons unsalted butter
1 medium onion, chopped
1-1/2 cups Arborio rice

1/2 cups Simi Chardonnay
4 to 5 cups chicken stock
1 cup freshly grated Asiago cheese
Optional garnish: sage sprigs and
*   radicchio leaves*

Preheat the oven to 350 degrees. Slice off the top 1/2 inch of the pumpkin and scoop out the seeds. Sprinkle salt and pepper into the cavity. Put one sage leaf in each pumpkin, replace the lid, and bake in a pan until just tender, 30 to 35 minutes. When the pumpkins are cool, discard the sage leaves. Remove the flesh of the pumpkin to a bowl. Make sure to leave enough flesh in the shell to prevent it from collapsing. Set pumpkins aside.

Heat the chicken stock until it is just simmering. In a heavy-bottomed pot, melt the butter and cook the onion over medium heat until translucent. Add the rice, stirring to coat. Add the Chardonnay and cook until the wine has been absorbed. Begin adding enough hot stock just to cover the rice, keeping liquid bubbling gently. Continue adding stock as it is absorbed into the rice, stirring with each addition.

Return the pumpkin shells to the oven to reheat. Cut the remaining 8 sage leaves into chiffonade. Test rice by tasting it. It should be al dente, and the sauce should look creamy. You may not need the entire stock. Stir in the chiffonade and correct the seasonings. Add in the reserved pumpkin flesh. Spoon risotto into the pumpkin shells. Prop the pumpkin top against the side, sprinkle with grated cheese and serve immediately, garnished with sage sprigs and radicchio, if desired.

Serves 8 as a first course.

© *Mary Evely, Executive Chef, Simi Winery.*

Serve with Simi Chardonnay.

Simi Winery

Tom's Yellow Tomato Ketchup

*10 large ripe yellow tomatoes
  (5 pounds)*
*2 large yellow peppers, seeded and
  chopped*
2 onions, chopped
10 cloves garlic, chopped
1 cup white wine vinegar
Juice and grated zest of 1/4 lemon
3/4 cup granulated sugar

1-1/2 teaspoons salt
2 teaspoons mustard seeds
1 tablespoon black peppercorns
1 tablespoon coriander seeds
1 teaspoon whole cloves
1 inch of a cinnamon stick
*1 inch of ginger, peeled and cut into
  4 slices*

Blanch tomatoes in boiling water for 30 seconds. Plunge into ice water. Remove the skins. Cut in half and remove seeds. Place tomatoes, peppers, onions, garlic, 1/2 cup of the vinegar, and the lemon juice and zest in a stainless-steel saucepan. Cook over medium heat until vegetables are cooked through, about 20 minutes.

Using a blender or food processor, coarsely purée and return to pan. Add the sugar, salt, and remaining vinegar.

In an 8-inch square of cheesecloth, put the mustard seeds, peppercorns, coriander seeds, cloves, cinnamon stick, and the ginger. Tie it up to form a spice bag and add it to the saucepan. Over low heat, simmer the vegetable mixture until thickened, taking care that it does not burn. It will take one to two hours, depending on what consistency you like for your ketchup. Serve with your favorite burger.

Makes about 2 quarts.

Serve with Seghesio Zinfandel or Sangiovese.

Simoneau Vineyards

Roasted Chicken with Cornbread Stuffing and Ginger-Spiced Peach Glaze

Stuffing:
2 strips bacon, chopped
1 shallot, peeled and chopped
1/2 cup dried peaches or apricots,
  roughly chopped
1/2 cup Hanna Chardonnay
3/4 cup crumbled leftover cornbread,
  or 2 pieces French bread, cubed
1 tablespoon dried sage
1/4 cup toasted chopped almonds
1/2 cup chicken stock
(Additional stock if needed)
Salt and pepper to taste

Glaze:
1/2 cup peach chutney (available in
grocery stores)
1/2-inch piece fresh ginger, peeled and
minced
2 tablespoons balsamic vinegar
2 tablespoons soy sauce

Chicken:
1 3-1/2- to 4-pound chicken
2 cloves garlic, peeled and minced
Salt and pepper to taste
Butcher's string for trussing

For the stuffing: In a medium sauté pan over medium heat, add the bacon and sauté until golden, but still slightly soft. Remove the bacon with a slotted spoon and set on a paper towel to drain. Pour off some of the excess bacon grease and return the pan to the heat. Add the shallots and sauté until softened and translucent. Add the peaches, deglaze the pan with wine, and simmer until 1/2 of the liquid remains. Add the remaining ingredients, adding more stock if necessary for desired consistency. Remove from heat and set aside to cool.

For the glaze: In a small saucepan, combine all of the ingredients and bring to a boil. Remove from heat and set aside.

For the chicken: Rinse the chicken and pat dry. Rub with garlic and season with salt and pepper. Stuff the inner cavity with the reserved stuffing, truss and set on a rack in a roasting pan. Place in the oven and roast for 1 hour and 15 minutes, basting every 15 minutes with the reserved glaze. Remove from the oven and set aside for 10 minutes before carving.

Serves 4.

Serve with Hanna Russian River Valley Elias Chardonnay.

Hanna Winery

Fig and Arugula Salad

Vinaigrette Dressing:
1 shallot, finely diced
1 tablespoon balsamic vinegar
1 teaspoon White Oak Chardonnay
2 to 3 tablespoons olive oil
Salt

1/3 cup pecans, toasted
6 ripe figs, beginning to show milky
  seams in their skins
2 large handfuls of arugula (set aside
  blossoms if available)
2 ounces creamy goat cheese, crumbled
Freshly ground pepper

Prepare the dressing by combining the shallot, vinegar, wine and pinch of salt in a bowl, then whisk in the olive oil.

Heat oven to 300 degrees. Place pecans in shallow pie tin and toast for 8 to 10 minutes; cool. Put aside. Quarter the figs. Wash and dry the arugula, place in bowl, then toss with the vinaigrette to lightly coat the arugula. Arrange the arugula on two plates, lay the figs and pecans equally between the two plates. Crumble goat cheese and spoon remaining vinaigrette over the top. Garnish with the arugula blossoms, if available, and dust with pepper.

Serves 2.

Serve with White Oak Chardonnay.

White Oak Vineyards and Winery

Baked Ham with Dijon Mustard

1-1/2 cups whole grain Dijon mustard
1/2 cup golden brown sugar
3 tablespoons dried marjoram
2 tablespoons minced garlic
2 tablespoons frozen orange juice
   concentrate, thawed

1 teaspoon ground black pepper
1 (9- to 1 0-pound) fully cooked bone-
   in-ham shank or butt end
2-1/2 cups Madeira wine
1 cup orange juice
2 teaspoons dried marjoram

Preheat oven to 400 degrees.

Mix first six ingredients in a medium bowl. Line large roasting pan with double layer of foil. Trim rind on ham, leaving 1/4-inch thick layer of fat. Using a sharp knife, score fat in 1-inch-wide diamond pattern. Place ham in prepared pan. Pour Madeira and 1 cup of orange juice into bottom of pan. Bake ham until heated through, about 45 minutes. Remove pan from oven.

Increase oven temperature to 450 degrees. Spread mustard mixture over top and sides of ham. Return to oven and bake until mustard coating is golden brown, about 35 minutes. Transfer ham to platter.

Skim fat from pan juices and discard. Pour pan juices into medium saucepan. Add marjoram and bring to boil. Season sauce with salt and pepper. Slice ham and serve with sauce.

Serves 8.

Serve with Field Stone Gewürztraminer.

Field Stone Winery

Sonoma County Olive Harvest Lamb

1 leg of lamb, boned, about 5 pounds
* (preferably Sonoma County lamb)*
Kosher salt
Black pepper in a mill
Tapenade (recipe follows)
10 rosemary sprigs, 6 to 8 inches long

2 pounds waxy-fleshed potatoes
1/2 pound carrots, in 2-inch pieces
6 to 8 shallots
15 garlic cloves, unpeeled
1/2 cup extra-virgin olive oil

Heat the oven to 450 degrees. Place the leg of lamb on a work surface, fat side up. Remove the fell (the thin outer covering), if any, and as much fat as possible. Season with salt and pepper. Turn the leg over and spread the tapenade over the inside. Roll up the leg around the tapenade to make a long package, pressing the roll tightly together as you do so, and tie up the roll with butcher's twine. Tuck 6 of the rosemary sprigs under the twine.

Place the potatoes, carrots, shallots, and garlic in a roasting pan, season with salt and pepper, and drizzle with half of the olive oil. Place a rack over the vegetables, set the lamb on the rack, and drizzle the remaining olive oil over the meat. Place in the oven and immediately reduce the heat to 350 degrees. Cook 1-1/4 to 1-1/2 hours to rare (15 to 20 minutes per pound), with an inside temperature of 120 degrees, which will continue to rise after the lamb is out of the oven.

Remove the lamb and vegetables from the oven and let them rest for 15 minutes. Using a slotted spoon, transfer the vegetables to a serving bowl. Remove the rosemary sprigs and the twine from the lamb, cut the lamb into 1/4-inch-thick slices, and arrange the slices on a serving platter. Some of the tapenade will probably fall out as you slice the lamb; place it in the center of the platter. Season with several turns of pepper, garnish with the remaining rosemary sprigs, and serve immediately, with the vegetables alongside.

Serves 6 to 9.

Tapenade:

1 cup Kalamata olives, pitted	*1 tablespoon Italian parsley*
1 cup cracked green olives, pitted	*2 anchovy fillets, rinsed*
1-1/2 cups Niçoise olives, pitted	*1/3 cup extra-virgin olive oil*
6 garlic cloves, minced	*Black pepper in a mill*

Using a very sharp knife (not a food processor), finely mince the olives, place them in a mixing bowl, and toss with the garlic and parsley. Pound the anchovies, using a mortar and pestle, until they form a paste. Add the paste to the olives, pour in the olive oil, grind in black pepper, and toss together lightly. Let the tapenade sit for 30 minutes before using.

Serves 6 to 9.

Serve with 1998 Clos du Bois Alexander Valley Reserve Merlot or 1998 Clos du Bois Alexander Valley Reserve Cabernet Sauvignon.

Chef Michele Anna Jordan offers this Sonoma County recipe from her tenth book, **California Home Cooking** *(Harvard Common Press, 1997), celebrating the other harvest, olives, which takes place just after the last grapes have been picked.*

Clos du Bois Winery

Fettucine with Kalamata Olives, Sundried Tomatoes, Asparagus and Asiago Cheese

1 cup sundried tomatoes, finely minced
8 tablespoons AVV Manzanillo olive
  oil
6 cloves garlic, chopped
1 cup olives, chopped

1 bunch asparagus, cut in 1-inch
  slices
1/2 cup grated Asiago cheese
4 ounces fettucine pasta

Place sundried tomatoes in saute pan with 1 cup water. Bring to a boil, reduce heat to simmer and let the dried tomatoes soften. Remove tomatoes from pan using a slotted spoon and chop, reserving 1/2 cup of the water.

Put tomatoes and asparagus back in pan with 1/2 cup water and bring to a boil. Cook asparagus until done, about 2 minutes. When most of the water evaporates and the tomatoes start to stick to the bottom of the pan, add 4 tablespoons of olive oil and the chopped garlic and cook. Next add the olives and 4 more tablespoons of olive oil.

Bring a large pot of salted water to boil and cook fettucine until al dente. Drain and place in the first pan with 1/2 cup grated Asiago cheese. Toss well and serve immediately.

Serves 2.

Enjoy with a glass of Wetzel Family Estate 1999 Chardonnay or 1998 Syrah.

Alexander Valley Vineyards

Taglierini with Sautéed Truffles

3 to 5 ounces black truffles (fresh or canned)
2 tablespoons olive oil
3 tablespoons minced shallots
1/2 cup ripe tomatoes, peeled, seeded and diced

4 tablespoons butter
Salt and freshly ground white pepper
1 pound taglierini pasta
Small, fresh basil leaves

Thinly peel the truffles, then cut them into paper-thin slices, using a truffle slicer, if available. Heat oil in a small frying pan and cook shallots until very soft and translucent. Add diced tomatoes, sauté briefly, and remove pan from heat.

Melt butter in a second frying pan, add sliced truffles and fry briefly on both sides. Season with salt and pepper.

Cook pasta in boiling water until al dente; drain and mix immediately with truffles and tomato. Transfer to four pre-warmed plates and garnish with basil leaves.

Serves 4.

Recipe by Don Bodio, Trentadue Winery.

Serve with Trentadue 1996 Alexander Valley Merlot.

Trentadue Winery

Soufflé-Broccoli

1-3/4 cups cooked broccoli
1-1/2 cups hot milk
3/4 teaspoon salt
1/4 teaspoon pepper

1/8 teaspoon nutmeg
1/4 cup soft butter or margarine
3 tablespoons flour
6 eggs, separated

Heat oven to 350 degrees.

Butter 2-quart casserole or soufflé dish. Put cooked broccoli in a blender and blend until smooth. Put in saucepan. Put milk, salt, pepper, nutmeg, butter, flour, and egg yolks in blender. Blend until smooth. Add to broccoli. Cook until thick. Cool. Beat egg whites until stiff. Carefully fold into broccoli mixture. Pour into prepared casserole dish. Bake 25 minutes, or until browned and puffed. Serve immediately.

Serves 6 to 8.

Vail Vista Vineyards

Baked Ziti with Spinach and Tomatoes

3/4 pound hot Italian sausages, casings removed
1 medium onion, chopped
3 large garlic cloves, chopped
1 (28-ounce) can diced, peeled tomatoes
1/4 cup purchased pesto sauce
10 ounces (about 3 cups) ziti or penne pasta, freshly cooked

8 cups (about 2/3 of a 10-ounce package) ready-to-use spinach leaves
6 ounces Mozzarella cheese, cubed
1 cup (about 3 ounces) grated Parmesan cheese

Heat heavy large saucepan over medium-high heat Add sausage, onion, and garlic and sauté until sausage is cooked through, about 10 minutes, breaking up meat with back of spoon. Add tomatoes with juices to pan. Simmer until sauce thickens slightly, stirring occasionally, about 10 minutes. Stir in pesto. Season sauce with salt and pepper.

Preheat oven to 375 degrees. Lightly oil 13 x 9-inch baking dish. Combine pasta, spinach, Mozzarella and 1/3 cup Parmesan cheese in large bowl. Stir in hot tomato sauce. Transfer mixture to prepared baking dish. Sprinkle with remaining 2/3 cup Parmesan cheese. Bake until sauce bubbles and cheeses melt, about 30 minutes. Serve with tossed green salad and garlic French bread.

Serves 10.

Serve with Sausal Private Reserve Zinfandel.

Sausal Winery

Crab Cakes

1 pound of crab meat
3 slices of toasted bread, crumbled
3 tablespoons of melted butter
1 teaspoon of Worcestershire sauce
5 drops of hot sauce

2 tablespoons of prepared mustard
1/2 teaspoon of salt
1/4 teaspoon of pepper
1 beaten egg

Mix well. Form into flat cakes and fry quickly on each side in hot oil (not olive oil) or bacon fat, or bake the cakes in a 350-degree oven for 20 minutes.

Southern Spoon Bread

Crab cakes or any type of fish is delicious with Southern Spoon Bread, sometimes called batter bread.

1-1/2 cups white cornmeal
1/2 teaspoon baking soda
1/2 teaspoon baking powder
1/2 teaspoon salt
1/2 teaspoon sugar

3 eggs
1 cup buttermild
1 cup sweet milk
2 tablespoons melted butter

While you are mixing the ingredients, preheat the oven to 350 degrees. Heat a buttered soufflé dish in the oven while the ingredients are being mixed. In a separate bowl, beat the egggs until thick and frothy and add to the eggs 1 cup of buttermilk and 1 cup of sweet milk with 2 tablespoons of melted butter. Pour this onto the cornmeal and mix it quickly and lightly with a slotted spoon. Pour the batter into the heated dish and bake for 45 minutes. Serve immediately.

Serves 6.

Serve with a glass of Wetzel Family Estate 1999 Chardonnay.

Maggie Wetzel, Alexander Valley Vineyards

Chicken with Italian Sauce

*6 large chicken breast halves,
  including skin and bones*
5 tablespoons olive oil
*1 large bell pepper, cut into half-inch
  pieces*
1 pound fresh mushrooms, sliced

1 clove fresh garlic, minced
2 cups chopped onions
1 cup dry, red wine
1 cup chicken broth
*1 teaspoon each: fresh basil, oregano,
  and thyme, finely chopped*

Preheat oven to 350 degrees. Heat 2 tablespoons oil in large skillet over medium heat. Add chicken breasts, skin side down. Add salt and pepper, garlic and herbs. Sauté until skin is browned. Transfer chicken, skin side up, into 15 x 10 x 2-inch glass baking dish.

Heat remaining 3 tablespoons oil in the same skillet over medium heat. Add bell pepper, mushrooms, garlic, and onions. Sauté until vegetables are tender and mushrooms begin to brown. Add wine and boil for 2 minutes. Add herbs and chicken broth; bring to a boil. Pour over chicken and cover dish with foil. Bake for 25 minutes. Uncover and bake for another 15 minutes, or until chicken is cooked through and sauce has thickened.

Serves 6.

Serve with Geyser Peak Cabernet.

Geyser Peak Winery

Scallop Pasta Sauce
with Olive Oil, Garlic and Hot Pepper

1 pound fresh bay or deep sea scallops
1/2 cup extra virgin olive oil
1 tablespoon garlic, chopped very fine
2 tablespoons chopped parsley
Chopped hot red chili pepper, to taste

Salt
1 to 1-1/2 pounds pasta, cooked
  according to package directions
1/2 cup dry, unflavored bread crumbs,
  lightly toasted in oven or skillet

Wash the scallops in cold water, pat thoroughly dry with a cloth towel, and cut up into pieces about 3/8-inch thick. Put the olive oil and garlic in a saucepan, turn on the heat to medium, and cook, stirring, until the garlic becomes colored a light gold. Add the parsley and hot pepper. Stir once or twice, then add the scallops and one or two large pinches of salt.

Turn the heat up to high and cook for about 1-1/2 minutes, stirring frequently, until the scallops lose their shine and turn a flat white. Do not overcook the scallops or they will become tough. If the scallops should shed a lot of liquid, remove them from the pan with a slotted spoon, and boil down the watery juices. Return the scallops to the pan, turn them over quickly, then turn off the heat.

Toss thoroughly with cooked, drained spaghettini (spaghetti). Add the bread crumbs, toss again, and serve at once.

Serves 6 to 8.

Recipe by Peter Seghesio, Jr.

Serve with Seghesio Pinot Grigio.

Seghesio Family Vineyards

Chicken with Chili Cream

4 boneless chicken breasts
4 cups fresh corn
1 onion, chopped
1 fresh green chili pepper, peeled,
  seeded and chopped

1/4 cup parsley, chopped
1/2 teaspoon cumin
1/4 cup half-and-half
1-1/4 cups chicken stock

Season chicken breasts lightly with salt and pepper. Arrange them in a single layer in a baking pan. Put corn, onion, chili pepper, parsley, cumin, and stock in a bowl and mix. Scatter half of this mix over the chicken and bake for 25 minutes in a preheated 325-degree oven. Simmer the remaining mix on low heat to cook and reduce. Put reduced mixture in a blender with the half-and-half and blend until smooth. Serve chicken with the baked vegetables and top with the blended sauce.

Serves 4.

Serve with Chateau Souverain Reserve Chardonnay or Geyser Peak Shiraz.

Chalk's Bend Vineyard

Baked Pear Bread Pudding

4 tablespoons soft sweet butter
6 slices day-old white bread
2/3 cup granulated sugar
1 teaspoon cinnamon
1-1/2 cups diced ripe pears

4 eggs
2 cups milk
1 teaspoon vanilla extract
3 tablespoons brown sugar

Preheat oven to 350 degrees. Spread 1 tablespoon butter over bottom and side of 1-1/2 quart, shallow baking dish. Trim crusts from bread. Spread slices with remaining butter. Sprinkle with 3 tablespoons granulated sugar, mixed with 3/4 teaspoon cinnamon. Cut into 1/2-inch cubes. Arrange one-half of the bread in prepared baking dish; top with diced pear. Add remaining bread crumbs.

In medium bowl, combine eggs, milk, vanilla, and remaining sugar. Mix until well blended. Pour over bread and pear. Set baking dish in shallow baking pan, pour hot water to 1-inch depth around dish. Bake 45 minutes. Sprinkle brown sugar mixed with remaining 1/4 teaspoon cinnamon over top. Bake 10 to 15 minutes, or until knife inserted in center comes out clean. Let cool on wire rack about 30 minutes. Serve warm.

Serves 8.

Serve with deLorimier "Lace" Late Harvest Sémillon.

deLorimier Winery

Spiced Walnuts

3 cups walnuts
2 tablespoons vegetable oil
1 teaspoon ground cumin

1/4 teaspoon cayenne pepper
2 tablespoons sugar
1 teaspoon salt

Preheat oven to 300 degrees. Place the nuts in a bowl.

Pour the oil into a small, heavy saucepan and place over medium-low heat until warm. Add the cumin and cayenne and stir until the mixture is aromatic, about 15 seconds. Pour the flavored oil over the nuts. Add the sugar and salt and stir to coat evenly. Transfer the nuts to a baking pan.

Bake, stirring occasionally, until the nuts are toasted, about 20 minutes. These are best served hot.

May be stored in an airtight container for up to 2 weeks. Reheat for about 5 minutes before serving.

Carameled Walnuts

3 to 4 cups walnut halves
1 teaspoon cinnamon
1 cup sugar

1/2 teaspoon salt
1/3 cup milk

Pour into large skillet, mix until caramelized (about 5 minutes). Quickly add 3 to 4 cups walnuts. Mix and turn out on foil.

Serves many.

Serve with deLorimier "Lace."

deLorimier Winery

Winter Recipes

Dried Figs with Blue Cheese and Bacon

1/4 pound dried, black Mission figs
1/4 cup Port
1/4 cup water

1/8 pound Maytag blue cheese, or
other high-quality blue cheese
3 to 4 thinly sliced slices apple-
smoked bacon

Trim the stems off the figs and cut in half lengthwise. In a small saucepan, over medium heat, gently simmer the figs in the Port and water for approximately 10 minutes, or until the figs are softened. Stir occasionally and watch to see that the liquid doesn't completely evaporate. Add water, if necessary. Remove figs with a slotted spoon and set Port cooking liquid aside.

Make an indentation in the cut side of each fig with your finger, or using the back of a small spoon. Place an approximate 1/2 teaspoon "nugget" of blue cheese in each fig pocket (it's okay for the cheese to mound above the surface). Place all the stuffed figs, cheese side up, on a foil-lined baking sheet.

Cut the bacon slices into 1-1/2-inch squares and drape one piece over each fig. Broil figs in a preheated broiler for approximately 3 minutes, or until bacon is cooked and the cheese is bubbly. Check to make sure they don't over-crisp. Serve warm with a toothpick or little skewer stuck in each one. Optional: Drizzle a few drops of reduced Port cooking liquid over each fig.

Makes approximately 12 hors d'oeuvres.

Jimtown Store

Bruschetta

12 slices French bread, about 1/2-inch
    thick
1/4 cup olive oil
2 medium tomatoes, chopped
2 cloves garlic, finely chopped

2 tablespoons capers, drained and
    chopped
Salt
Pepper

Heat oven to 375 degrees. Place bread slices on an ungreased cookie sheet. Drizzle oil over each slice. Bake until golden brown. While bread is toasting, mix remaining ingredients. Spoon tomato mixture over the bread slices.

Serves 12.

Serve with Geyser Peak Merlot.

Geyser Peak Winery

Taco Soup

1 large can peeled and diced tomatoes
1 small can peeled and diced tomatoes
1 can diced green chilis
1 can pinto beans
1 can whole kernel corn
1 pound ground beef

1 small onion, chopped
Olive oil
1 package Taco Seasoning mix
1 package Ranch Dressing mix
2 to 3 cloves garlic, minced

Brown the beef and onion in olive oil and add Taco and Ranch seasoning mixes. Add all the canned vegetables (do not drain). Mix well and simmer for 20 minutes. Serve in bowls with shredded Cheddar cheese on top. Serve with garlic French bread and a green salad.

Serves 6.

Serve with a Merlot.

Nancy Dalziel
Ellis Ranch

Wild Mushroom Soup

12 tablespoons butter
3/4 cup onions, chopped into 1/2-inch
  pieces
3/4 cup celery, chopped into 1/2-inch
  pieces
1-1/2 cups potatoes, peeled and cut
  into 1/2-inch pieces
1 cup leeks (white part only), chopped
  into 1/2-inch pieces
3 whole bay leaves

3 tablespoons freshly chopped parsley
  stems (no leaves)
1 tablespoon fresh thyme
6 whole garlic cloves, peeled
8 cups vegetable or chicken stock
2 pounds fresh wild mushrooms (gold
  chanterelles, oyster, shiitake and
  black trumpet all do well)
2 cups cream
Salt and pepper to taste

Melt 8 tablespoons of the butter in a thick-bottomed saucepan. Add the onions, celery, potatoes, and leeks. Cover and cook for a few minutes, making sure not to brown them. Add the bay leaves, parsley stems, and thyme, along with the garlic cloves; stir and cover. Cook at a low heat for about 15 minutes, controlling the heat so they do not take on any color. Uncover and let some of the liquid that has formed evaporate (turn the heat up a little to help this along). Pour in the stock, bring to a boil and simmer this base for 30 minutes.

Season mushrooms with salt and pepper. Sauté in 3 tablespoons butter at high heat until just tender. Place the mushrooms into the soup base after it has cooked about 30 minutes, as mentioned. The cream may be reduced by half and also added. At this time, the soup may be seasoned with salt and pepper to your liking. Blend the soup and strain the purée through a strainer that is not too fine. The last tablespoon of butter may be stirred in at the end. Garnish with either chopped chives or Italian parsley.

Serves 8.

Recipe by Martin W. Courtman, Executive Chef, Chateau Souverain.

Serve with Chateau Souverain Reserve Chardonnay.

Chateau Souverain

Hearty Cauliflower Soup

1-1/2 cups potato chunks
4 cups light broth
5 cups cauliflower pieces
1 large onion, chopped
1 clove garlic
2 tablespoons olive oil

1 cup Sauvignon Blanc
White pepper
Salt
Optional vegetables: roasted red
*   pepper strips, fresh corn, sautéed*
*   mushrooms, sautéed asparagus*
*   slices, 1-1/2 to 2 inches long*

Cook the potatoes in the broth (peel first for lighter-colored soup). Sauté cauli-flower, garlic, and onion in olive oil until lightly browned and soft. When potato is fully cooked, add the cauliflower mixture to the potatoes. Blend potatoes, cauliflower, and broth in blender until smooth.

This is done best in small batches. Return to stove, add the wine, and add desired optional vegetables. (Do not blend optional vegetables.)

Serves 8.

Serve with Chateau Souverain or Geyser Peak Sauvignon Blanc.

Chalk's Bend Vineyard

Chicken with Glazed Onions

1 *roasting chicken, about 3-1/2 pounds*
2 *teaspoons tarragon*
3 *lemons*
1/4 *cup unsalted butter, melted*
2 *tablespoons Dijon mustard*

4 *yellow onions, cut in half crosswise*
2 *tablespoons balsamic vinegar*
1/2 *cup canned chicken stock*
Salt and pepper to taste

Preheat oven to 375 degrees. Sprinkle cavity of chicken with 1 teaspoon of the tarragon. Cut one of the lemons in quarters and distribute in the cavity. Squeeze remaining lemons for about 1/4 cup juice. Stir juice, remaining tarragon and mustard into small saucepan with melted butter. Mix well. Brush some of the butter mixture over chicken and place breast side down in a shallow roasting pan. Place onion halves around chicken and brush amply with butter mixture.

Place in oven to roast.

At the end of 30 minutes, spoon vinegar over onions and add stock to roasting pan. Baste chicken with pan juices and roast for another 30 minutes. Turn chicken breast side up and baste with remaining butter mixture. Season with salt and pepper and continue to roast another 20 to 30 minutes, or until chicken is tender and golden brown. Serve with lumpy mashed potatoes.

For those of you who own a Weber Bar-B-Que, this chicken is also excellent cooked by the indirect heat method.

Serves 4

Serve with Stuhlmuller Vineyards Chardonnay.

Stuhlmuller Vineyards

Lamb Shanks Braised in "Sin Zin" Zinfandel

6 lamb shanks
Flour for dredging
1/4 cup extra-virgin olive oil
1/2 bottle Alexander Valley Sin Zin
1 tablespoon Timber Crest Farms
  Sundried Tapenade
1 onion, sliced
4 carrots, diced

4 large cloves of garlic
1 tablespoon fresh oregano, chopped
2 cups chicken broth
1 cup peeled, seeded and diced
  tomatoes
Salt and pepper to taste

Heat oil in pot large enough to hold 6 lamb shanks. Place flour seasoned with salt and pepper in paper bag, add lamb and shake, coating lamb well. Remove from bag and shake off excess flour. Place lamb in preheated pan and brown completely. Next add onion, carrots, garlic and oregano and cook for 5 minutes. Add wind, sundried tomato tapenade, chicken broth and fresh tomatoes. Bring to a simmer and cook for 2 hours. Thicken sauce to desired thickness with 1 or 2 tablespoons cornstarch mixed with equal amount of wine or water. Let sauce simmer for 5 minutes after adding cornstarch.

This is a good mead to do the day before so the flavors can mellow together. Serve over soft polenta or saffron risotto.

Serves 6.

Serve with Alexander Valley Vineyards 1999 "Sin Zin" Sinfandel or Alexander Valley 1998 Syrah.

Alexander Valley Vineyards

Roasted Red Bell Pepper Bisque
with Shrimp and Romano Cheese

5 large red bell peppers
3-1/2 cups chicken stock
1 teaspoon paprika
1 teaspoon sugar
3/4 cup whipping cream
1/2 cup grated Pecorino Romano
* cheese*

Hot pepper sauce
1 tablespoon olive oil
16 large uncooked shrimp, peeled,
* deveined and coarsely chopped*
3 tablespoons thinly sliced fresh basil

Char red bell peppers over gas flame or in broiler until blackened on all sides. Enclose in paper bag. Let stand 10 minutes. Peel and seed peppers. Cut 1 pepper into matchstick-sized strips and set aside. Coarsely chop remaining 4 peppers. Combine chopped peppers and stock in heavy, large saucepan. Bring to boil, reduce heat and simmer until peppers are very tender, about 5 minutes.

Working in batches, purée soup in blender until smooth. Return purée to saucepan. Mix in paprika and sugar. Simmer 5 minutes to blend flavors. Whisk in cream and Pecorino Romano cheese. Season to taste with hot pepper sauce, salt, and pepper.

Heat 1 tablespoon oil in medium skillet over medium-high heat. Add reserved bell pepper strips and shrimp. Sauté until shrimp are cooked through, about 3 minutes. Season with salt and pepper. Divide shrimp mixture among four bowls. Rewarm soup; ladle around shrimp mixture. Sprinkle basil over top and serve.

Serves 4.

Recipe by Don Bodio, Trentadue Winery.

Serve with Trentadue 1999 Alexander Valley Merlot Rosé.

Trentadue Winery

Macaroni and Cheese

1 pound macaroni
1 teaspoon butter
1 egg, beaten
1 teaspoon salt
1 teaspoon dry mustard

1 tablespoon hot water
1 cup milk
3 cups shredded cheese (sharp is best)
1 pound Little Smokies (drained)

Cook macaroni until tender, then drain. Stir in butter and egg. Mix salt and mustard with hot water, then add to milk. Add cheese, reserve enough to sprinkle on top. Mix the milk/cheese mixture with macaroni and mix in the Little Smokies. Sprinkle with remaining cheese. Bake in a 350-degree oven for 45 minutes, or until custard is set.

Serves 6.

Serve with Fetzer "Barrel Select" Merlot.

Linda Lynch Graperfection

Cheese Fondue

1 pound Gruyere
1/2 pound Appenzeller
1/2 pound Fontina d'Aosta
1/2 pound Comte

3 tablespoons flour
1 garlic clove, cut in half
2 cups Chardonnay
2 sour baguettes

Cut the baguettes in half lengthwise and then in small slices. Put aside.

Grate the cheeses into a large bowl. Toss with the flour. Rub fondue pot with cut side of garlic. Put wine in pot and bring to a slow boil. Turn heat to medium and add cheese by handfuls, stirring in a figure eight. Keep wine at a simmer. Takes about 15 minutes until it thickens a bit. Grate fresh pepper on top. Serve immediately with cut pieces of French bread.

Serves 8.

Serve with Chardonnay.

Hafner Vineyard

Lamb Chops in Red Wine

8 lamb rib chops, cut about 1-inch thick
1 teaspoon salt
1/2 teaspoon pepper
2 tablespoons butter

2 tablespoons olive oil
1/2 cup Sausal Zinfandel
1 teaspoon dried thyme
2 tablespoons chopped fresh parsley

Trim excess fat from chops. Pound chops between two pieces of waxed paper or plastic wrap, being careful not to separate meat from bone, until meat is flattened to about 1/4-inch thickness. Season on both sides with salt and pepper.

In a large frying pan, melt 1 tablespoon butter with 1 tablespoon olive oil over medium heat. Add chops and cook, turning once, 4 to 6 minutes, or until barely pink in center. Remove chops to plate and cover with foil to keep warm. Repeat with remaining chops, adding more butter as needed.

Add wine and thyme to pan. Boil over high heat, scraping up browned bits from bottom of pan, until reduced to about 2 tablespoons, 2 to 3 minutes. Add parsley. Pour sauce over chops.

Serves 4.

Serve with Sausal Private Reserve Zinfandel.

Sausal Winery

Beef Stroganoff

*1 pound round steak, cut in long, thin
    strips*
1/2 cup chopped onions
2 tablespoons olive oil
3 tablespoons butter

3 tablespoons flour
1 (14-ounce) can beef consommé
1 can mushrooms
1 cup sour cream
3 tablespoons Sherry

Brown meat and onions in olive oil in frying pan. Remove from pan and set aside. Drain oil. In the same pan, melt 3 tablespoons butter. Slowly stir in flour and blend well before adding consommé a little at a time. Mix well. Add mushrooms, cream, catsup, and Sherry.

Blend well, stirring until sauce has thickened. Add meat and onions. Heat. Serve over rice or noodles.

Serves 6.

Wasson Vineyards

Chicken Chardonnay

4 ounces sweet butter
1 clove garlic, minced
1/4 cup shallots, minced
1 teaspoon whole fennel seeds
1 cup Chardonnay
4 chicken breasts (2 whole), skinned,
  boned and lightly pounded flat
1/2 teaspoon salt

1/4 teaspoon white pepper
2 large cucumbers, peeled, cut in half
  lengthwise and seeded
1 cup plain yogurt
1 teaspoon cornstarch
12 cherry tomatoes
Salt and pepper to taste
2 tablespoons chopped parsley

In a large skillet with a lid, melt butter and add garlic, shallots, and fennel seeds. Sauté 2 minutes over medium heat. Add wine and bring to boil. Season chicken with salt and pepper and add to pan. Poach, covered, 3 to 4 minutes per side. Remove chicken to heated platter and keep warm. Reduce pan liquid by one-third.

Meanwhile, slice cucumbers into crescents about 1/4-inch wide. Add cucumbers to pan and poach, covered, about 5 minutes, until they are translucent but still crisp. Arrange on heated platter around chicken.

Place yogurt in a small bowl and whisk in cornstarch. Slowly whisk hot pan juices into the yogurt until well blended. Return sauce to the pan and whisk about 2 minutes over low heat, or until it thickens. Taste and adjust seasonings if necessary. Add tomatoes and heat until they are just warmed through. Pour sauce over chicken and vegetables. Sprinkle with chopped parsley.

Serves 4.

Serve with deLorimier Chardonnay.

deLorimier Winery

Pork Chops à la Piacenza

2 tablespoons butter
2 tablespoons olive oil
4 pork chops
Flour

4–6 sage leaves
Salt and pepper
1 cup canned, peeled chopped plum
   tomatoes*

Melt butter in olive oil over medium heat in pan large enough to hold four pork chops. Coat chops in flour and brown each side when butter starts to foam, and continue cooking 3 to 4 minutes.

Add sage leaves, salt, pepper and, chopped tomatoes. Lower heat to medium low. Cover and cook 1 hour, turning several times, or until chops are tender.

*If fresh plum tomatoes are used, slit a cross at one end, boil in water for 2–3 minutes until skin can be removed.

Serves 4

Serve with Silver Oak Cabernet Sauvignon

Silver Oak Cellars

Linguine with Clams

1 anchovy filet
1/4 teaspoon red pepper
2 to 3 cloves garlic, diced
1 to 2 shallots
2 crushed roma tomatoes
Parsley
Basil

1/4 cup white wine
1/2 cup tomato sauce
Salt and pepper (pinch)
Saffron (very little but critical)
1 dozen small clams
1/2 pound linguini pasta cooked
    according to package directions

Sauté anchovy, red pepper, garlic and shallots for 2 to 5 minutes in 1 to 2 table-spoons of olive oil on moderate heat. Add crushed roma tomatoes, cooking for 2 to 5 minutes, then add white wine, tomato sauce, salt, pepper, and saffron.

Scrub and soak clams, then add to sauce. Leave in sauce to simmer for about 15 minutes until shells open. (Discard any clams that do not open.) Serve over linguini.

Serves 2.

Recipe by Peter Seghesio.

Serve with '98 Seghesio Sangiovese.

Seghesio Family Vineyards

Simoneau Tourtiere (French-Canadian Meat Pie)

Brenda's Grandmother's Pie Crust:
3 cups flour
1 teaspoon salt
1 cup cold shortening or butter
1 beaten egg (in pie crust)
1/2 cup ice water
1 tablespoon vinegar
1 beaten egg (topping pie crust)

Meat Pie Filling:
5 to 6 medium potatoes
1 large onion, chopped
1/4 pound ground pork
1/4 pound ground round
1/4 teaspoon (or to taste) of each:
*   salt, pepper, sage, basil, and thyme*

For the Pie Crust: Blend flour and salt in a bowl. Cut in the shortening or butter. Add beaten egg, vinegar, and enough ice water so that dough comes together in a ball. Divide dough into three pieces. Flatten each piece into a small circle with the palm of your hand and wrap with plastic. Let two circles rest in refrigerator for 30 minutes (or until the next day) and freeze the third for another day.

For the Meat Pie Filling: Peel and boil potatoes in salted water until fork tender. Drain and place in a large bowl. While potatoes are cooling, brown meat in a skillet, remove, and drain off excess fat. Use the same pan to sauté onions until translucent. Add the cooked meat and the spices. Simmer for 5 minutes. Coarsely mash the potatoes. Stir in the onion and meat mixture. Let cool. Once cool, it's time to roll out the pie dough.

Set oven temperature at 375 degrees. Beat second egg and set aside. Roll out the two disks of pie dough to about 1/8-inch thick. Fit one piece of the pie dough into the bottom of a 9-inch pie plate. Fill with the chilled meat pie filling. Place second piece of dough on top, seal and crimp edges, cut a few holes in the top crust using the tip of a knife to let steam escape during baking. Brush the top of the pie with the beaten egg.

Bake for 40 to 45 minutes, or until crust is golden. You may want to cover with foil during the last 15 minutes so crust does not become too browned.

Serves 6 to 8.

Serve with Hanna Merlot or Jordan Cabernet Sauvignon.

Simoneau Coleslaw

1/4 cup mayonnaise
1/4 cup cider vinegar
1 tablespoon sugar
1 tablespoon poppy seeds

1 small head of green cabbage
5 medium carrots
1 small sweet onion, chopped small

Place mayonnaise, vinegar, sugar, and poppy seeds in a small bowl. Stir all ingredients together until well blended.

Remove outer leaves from and core the cabbage. Finely shred or chop. Place in a medium bowl. Peel and grate carrots. Add to cabbage and toss together. Add chopped onion and toss. Stir in just enough dressing to moisten the salad. Serve alongside your favorite grilled meat.

Serves 6.

Serve with a youthful Zinfandel like Chateau Souverain's.

Simoneau Vineyards

Alaskan King Salmon Chowder

1 tablespoon butter
2 medium leeks, chopped
2 garlic cloves, minced
1/2 cup yellow corn
1/4 cup chopped red bell peppers
1/2 cup White Oak Chardonnay
3 cups fish stock (or 1 cup clam juice
    and 2 cups chicken stock)

2 large red potatoes, diced with peel on
3/4-pound Alaskan King salmon filet,
    boned, skinned and cut into 1/2-inch
    pieces
1 cup heavy cream
Salt and pepper to taste
Garnish of fresh parsley, chives and
    croutons

Over medium-heat butter, sauté leeks, garlic, corn, and red peppers until tender, about 5 to 10 minutes. Do not brown. Add wine; simmer 5 minutes. Add stock and potatoes, cook over medium-high heat, 10 to 15 minutes. Add salmon and simmer 15 minutes. Add cream and reheat. Season with salt and pepper to taste. Garnish with parsley, chives and croutons.

Serves 6.

Serve with White Oak Sonoma County Chardonnay.

White Oak Vineyards and Winery

Venison Stew

3 pounds venison stew meat, cut into bite-sized pieces
1 cup flour
2 tablespoons salt
2 tablespoons pepper
Oil
3 cups chicken broth

1 head garlic
1 cup white wine
1 cup water
2 cups dried mushrooms
2 tablespoons vinegar
1/2 cup red wine

Preheat oven to 350 degrees. Put mushrooms into bowl of warm water to soften. When soft, cut into small pieces. Remove gristle from stew meat and dry well. In a large frying pan, heat oil. While oil is heating, place flour, salt, and pepper in a plastic bag. Add meat to flour mixture, a few pieces at a time. Shake off excess flour. Put floured meat into hot oil and brown all sides. When done, remove meat from pan and place on paper towels so excess oil will drain from meat.

Place chicken broth into a large, oven-safe, covered pan and add browned meat to broth along with sliced garlic and white wine. Bring to simmer and add water and cut-up mushrooms. Let simmer for about 15 minutes. Make sure all meat is covered by sauce; if not, add a little more liquid until all meat is covered. Cover stew and place into 350-degree oven. Check after 25 minutes and if stew is bubbling, turn down 25 degrees and repeat three times, making sure stew maintains a slow simmer. Taste; be sure meat is done. I do this the day before and finish the day of the dinner. Twenty minutes before serving, stir in red wine and vinegar. Serve over polenta and cheese.

Serves 6 to 8.

From Julio and Aileen Gallo family recipes.

Serve with 1996 Gallo of Sonoma Barrelli Creek Cabernet Sauvignon.

Gallo of Sonoma

Creamy Polenta with Italian Sausage

Instant polenta
4 Italian sausages
1 red bell pepper, cut in strips
2 garlic cloves
12 ounces Provolone cheese, sliced

1 cup Parmesan cheese, grated
4 tablespoons butter, cut up
1 jar pasta sauce or your favorite
  recipe

Follow directions on package for instant polenta, using 1/2 water and 1/2 milk for liquid. When almost done, add butter and cheese.

Meanwhile, poach Italian sausage in small covered pan with water. Sauté red pepper and garlic in 2 teaspoons olive oil.

When polenta is ready, **immediately** spread small amount on plate, top with Provolone cheese and another thin layer of polenta, pasta sauce, the red pepper and one sausage.

Serves 4.

Serve with Sausal Private Reserve Zinfandel.

Sausal Winery

California Christmas Risotto

1/4 cup dry white wine
1/4 cup dried tomato bits
2 tablespoons unsalted butter
1 tablespoon olive oil
1 small yellow onion, minced
1 shallot, minced
3 garlic cloves, minced
1-1/2 cups Arborio or Carnaroli rice
5 to 6 cups stock, hot
1/2 cup heavy cream

3 ounces California teleme cheese or
  3 ounces brie, cut into small pieces
Kosher salt
Black pepper in a mill
1/2 cup pine nuts, toasted
3 tablespoons minced Italian parsley
  or snipped chives
6 pieces dried tomatoes packed in oil,
  cut into thin strips

Bring the wine and the tomato bits to a boil in a non-reactive saucepan. Reduce the heat and simmer until the wine is reduced by one-third. Set the pan aside.

Heat the butter and the olive oil together in a large saucepan over medium heat. When the butter is melted, add the onion, and sauté it until it is soft and fragrant, about 8 minutes. Add the shallot and sauté for 5 minutes more. Add the garlic and sauté for 2 minutes more. Add the rice and stir with a wooden spoon until each grain begins to turn milky white, about 2 minutes. Keeping the stock hot over low heat, add the stock, 1/2 cup at a time, stirring after each addition until nearly all the liquid is absorbed. Continue to add stock and stir until the rice is tender, a total of 18 to 20 minutes.

After the last addition of stock, stir in the reserved tomato bits and wine and remove the pan from the heat. Stir in the cream and the cheese. Taste, season with salt and pepper, and stir in the pine nuts and half of the parsley or chives. Transfer the risotto to a serving platter or individual plates, garnish with the remaining parsley or chives and the tomato strips, and serve immediately.

Serves 4 to 6.

© *Michele Anna Jordan*

Serve with 1997 Clos du Bois Alexander Valley Reserve Tempranillo.

Clos du Bois Winery

Doreen Murphy's Irish Stew

1-1/2 pound cubed round steak
1-1/2 pound cubed lamb
Flour
Olive oil
3 onions, chopped
3 cups chopped celery
2 green peppers, chopped
4 cloves garlic, chopped

1 teaspoon beau monde
1 teaspoon dill weed
1 sprig parsley, chopped
1 cup beef stock
8 carrots, cut to size desired
8 potatoes, cut to size desired
Salt and pepper to taste

Roll meat in flour. Brown in olive oil. Remove meat and lightly sauté onions, celery, green peppers, and garlic. Place in stock pot with beef stock and seasoning. Cook slowly about 2 hours.

Add carrots and potatoes and cook 1 hour more (can add 1 cup of lager or Guinness or water as needed). Thicken with flour, cornstarch or cornmeal, if desired. Add salt and pepper as needed.

Serves 4.

Recipe by Doreen Murphy, Murphy-Goode Estate Winery.

Serve with Murphy-Goode Cabernet Sauvignon.

Murphy-Goode Estate Winery

Garlic Pork Tenderloin
with Roasted Red Bell Peppers

6 red bell peppers, large size
1/2 cup golden raisins
1/4 cup Hanna olive oil
3 tablespoons balsamic vinegar
2 large garlic cloves, minced
1-1/2 cups chopped green onions
1 cup Hanna olive oil
1/2 cup purchased barbecue sauce
1/3 cup white wine vinegar

3 tablespoons light soy sauce
2 tablespoons brown sugar
1 tablespoons green hot pepper sauce
2 teaspoons Worcestershire sauce
2 large garlic cloves, minced
1 tablespoon honey
1/2 teaspoon Lawry's seasoned salt
3 pounds pork tenderloins

Char peppers over gas flame, broiler, or BBQ until blackened on all sides. Wrap in paper bag and let stand 10 minutes. Peel, seed, and cut bell peppers into strips. Transfer peppers to medium bowl. Mix in raisins, olive oil, balsamic vinegar, and garlic. Cover and refrigerate. (May be prepared two days ahead. Let stand at room temperature two hours before using.)

Prepare marinade for pork, mixing all the remaining ingredients in a bowl, except the pork. Place pork in a shallow glass baking dish. Pour marinade over pork, cover and chill at least two hours and up to 12 hours. Prepare BBQ or preheat broiler. Remove pork from marinade and grill or broil, turning often, until meat thermometer registers 155 degrees. This takes about 20 minutes. Slice pork and arrange on platter. Spoon bell pepper-raisin mixture around the pork.

Serves 8.

Serve with a Hanna Russian River Valley Pinot Noir.

Hanna Winery

Sausage and Eggplant Scrabble

1 pound eggplant	*1 pound Italian sausage*
4 pieces of pancetta	*1/2 cup red wine*
2 onions, coarsely chopped	*1 cup chicken broth*
6 tablespoons olive oil	*2 tablespoons fresh thyme, chopped*
1/2 red pepper	*3 tablespoons fresh parsley, chopped*
1 (31-ounce) can of Italian tomatoes, drained	*2 garlic cloves, minced*

Cut eggplant into 1 to 1-1/2-inch cubes. Salt, put in strainer and let drain for 1 hour. Pat dry on paper towels. Put in pan in 450-degree oven with 4 tablespoons oil for 20 minutes or so until soft. Stir once or twice.

Cut up pancetta. Cook slowly in fry pan until browned. Drain on paper towel. Cook Italian sausage meat in large fry pan until done. Drain on paper towels. Cook chopped onions in 2 tablespoons oil in same pan until soft. Add chopped red pepper and sauté another 10 minutes. Add eggplant and and sausage to onion mix. Add cut up tomatoes. Add wine and chicken broth. Cover and simmer for 30 minutes. Take off top. Add garlic, parsley, thyme, and pancetta. Cook at a simmer for 15 minutes. Can be made ahead and reheated.

Serve on top of polenta. Make ahead and spread on cookie sheet. Cut into serving pieces, place on buttered cookie sheet and roast in 400-degree oven until good and hot. Sprinkle with grated imported Parmesan cheese after spooning sausage mix on top.

Serves 4 to 6.

Serve with Cabernet Sauvignon.

Hafner Vineyard

Onion Puff Pastry Tart

2 pounds mild onions
4 tablespoons unsalted butter
Salt and freshly ground white pepper
1/2 package (1 sheet) frozen puff
  pastry

2 egg yolks
1/4 cup cream
2 ounces Fontina cheese, grated

Peel and thinly slice onions. Cook very slowly in the butter, stirring occasionally until soft, about 30 minutes. Do not let them brown. Season to taste with salt and pepper. Defrost puff pastry and roll out to 1/8-inch thickness. For first course presentation, line a round tart pan and prick pastry with a fork.

For appetizers, cut into 3 strips about 3-1/2 inches wide. Lightly score pastry 1/4 inch in from edges and prick area inside, scoring with a fork. Bake for 15 to 20 minutes at 375 degrees, or until the pastry is lightly colored. Mix together the egg yolks, cream, and onions and spread over the pastry shell. Sprinkle cheese over the top, return to oven, and bake for an additional 20 minutes, or until filling is set and cheese is lightly browned. This tart is equally good served hot or at room temperature.

Serves 6 as a first course,
or 12 as an appetizer.

Although people happily consume this tart at any time of the year, the richness of the cream, egg, and cheese make it ideal for a chilly winter day.

© Mary Evely, Executive Chef, Simi Winery

Serve with Simi Chardonnay.

Simi Winery

Bünet

3/4 cup brown sugar	*Brandy, Rum, Kahlua or vanilla*
1 teaspoon water	*9 eggs*
1 round pan for baking	*4 cups milk*
12 to 14 macaroons	*9 tablespoons white sugar*

To make the caramel: Put the brown sugar and water in the pan you are going to bake with. Turn on the heat and melt the sugar until it is a dark brown color. Turn on the oven to 315 degrees. Dip the macaroons in brandy (or other flavors). Place around the sides of the pan.

Warm up the milk in a saucepan. Let it cool a little. Beat 9 eggs with a tablespoon of white sugar per egg, then add the milk. Combine with one of the flavorings, approximately 1 teaspoon. Put the eggs and milk in the baking pan.

Place a pan of warm water in the oven and place the baking pan in it. Bake one hour in oven. Test with a knife. If knife comes out dry, it is done. Take out of oven and let cool 10 to 15 minutes. Turn it over onto a pretty serving plate. May be served chilled or at room temperature.

Serves 6 to 12.

From the kitchen of Rachel Ann Seghesio (original recipe from family founder Angela Seghesio).

Serve with Seghesio Port.

Seghesio Family Vineyards

The Wineries of the Valley

Alexander Valley Vineyards
8644 Hwy 128, Healdsburg
P.O. Box 175, Healdsburg, CA 95448
(707) 433-7209 or (800) 888-7209
Open 10-5 daily; tours by appointment
Picnic tables
Varieties: CB,C,CY,PN,Z,CS,M,CF, G
www.avvwine.com

Canyon Road Winery
19550 Geyserville Ave., Geyserville (707)
857-3417 or (800) 793-9463
Varieties: CS,M,SB,L,V,JR
Open 10-5 daily
www.canyonroadwinery.com

Chateau Souverain
Independence Lane at Hwy. 101
P.O. Box 528, Geyserville, CA 95441
(707) 433-8281 or (888) 80-WINES
Open 10-5 daily
Complimentary tasting • Café
Gourmet lunch served daily
Dinner Fri-Sun
Indoor fireplace • Outdoor terrace dining •
Special events, limited
weddings, please call for information
Varieties: SB,C,V,Z,SYRAH,M,CS
www.chateausouverain.com

Clos du Bois
19410 Geyserville Ave., Geyserville
(707) 857-3100 or (800) 222-3189
Open 10-4:30 daily
Credit cards • Picnic area
Varieties: C,CS,M,ME,PN,SB,Z

deLorimier Winery
2001 Hwy 128, Geyserville
P.O. Box 487, Geyserville, CA 95441
(707) 857-2000 or (800) 546-7718
Open 10-4:30 daily
Varieties: SB,C,SG,M,CS,CF, Malbec, LH
Sémillon, Spectrum, Mosaic
www.delorimierwinery.com

Field Stone Winery
10075 Hwy 128, Healdsburg CA 95448
(707) 433-7266 or (800) 54GRAPE
Open 10-5 daily; tours by appointment
Picnic grounds • Special events
Varieties: CS, Reserve CS, C, Reserve C, SB,
Reserve Merlot, Reserve Petite Syrah (century-old vines), Reserve Viognier & "dry style" Gewürztraminer.
www.fieldstonewinery.com

Geyser Peak Winery
22280 Chianti Road, Geyserville
P.O Box 25, Geyserville, CA 95441
(800) 255-9463
Varieties: SB,C,JR,G,CS,M,SH,Z,CF, Dry
Riesling, Malbec, Rosé,
Sparkling Shiraz, Opulence, Rhone Style
Blend
Open 10-5 daily
www.geyserpeakwinery.com

C=Chardonnay, CS=Cabernet Sauvignon, M=Merlot, Z=Zinfandel, PN=Pinot Noir, SB=Sauvignon Blanc, V=Viognier, SG=Sangiovese, G=Gewürztraminer, ME=Meritage, FB=Fumé Blanc, CF=Cabernet Franc, SY=Syrah, PS=Petite Sirah, JR=Johannisberg Riesling, SH=Shiraz.

Hafner Vineyard
P.O. Box 1038, Healdsburg, CA 95448
(707) 433-4606
Visits by appointment only
Wines sold exclusively by mail to
reciprocal states.
Varieties: C, Reserve Chardonnay, CS
Wines are estate bottled.
e-mail hafnervnyd@aol.com

Hanna Winery
9280 Hwy 128, Healdsburg, CA 95448
(707) 431-4310 or (800) 854-3987
Open 10-4 daily
Large groups please call ahead
Picnic grounds • Special events
Varieties: SB,C,PN,Z,M,CS, Syrah
www.hannawinery.com

Hart's Desire Wines
25094 Asti Road, Cloverdale
Varieties: CS,CF,Z,C
(707) 579-1687; by appointment

Johnson's Alexander Valley Wines
8333 Hwy 128, Healdsburg, CA 95448
(707) 433-2319
Open 10-5 daily
Varieties: Z,PN,CS,C,PS & Johannesberg
Reisling
www.johnsonwines.com

Jordan Vineyard & Winery
1474 Alexander Valley Road
Healdsburg, CA 95448
P.O. Box 878, Healdsburg

(707) 431-5250 or (800) 654-1213
Varieties: C,C,
•Retail sales: M-F 8-5, Sat 9-5
•Tours by appointment only
e-mail: publicrelation@jordancos.com

Kendall-Jackson Wine Country Store
337 Healdsburg Ave.
Healdsburg, CA 95448
(707) 433-7102
Open 10-4:30 daily
Varieties: SB,C,V,FB,PN,SY,Z,M,CS,CF &
Reisling
www.kj.com

Murphy-Goode Estate Winery
4001 Hwy 128, Geyserville
P.O. Box 158, Geyserville, CA 95441
(707)-431-7644 or (800) 499-7644
Open 10:30-4:30 daily
Varieties: FB,C,PN,Z,M,CS,G, Petit Verdot,
Sauvignon Musque & Port

Sausal Winery
7370 Hwy 128, Healdsburg, CA 95448
(707) 433-2285 or (800) 500-2285
Open 10-4 daily • Picnic grounds
Varieties: Z,CS,SG, Proprietary
White Blend
www.sausalwinery.com

Seghesio Family Vineyards
14730 Grove Street
Healdsburg, CA 95448
(707) 433-7764
Open 10-4:30 daily

C=Chardonnay, CS=Cabernet Sauvignon, M=Merlot, Z=Zinfandel, PN=Pinot Noir, SB=Sauvignon Blanc, V=Viognier, SG=Sangiovese, G=Gewürztraminer, ME=Meritage, FB=Fumé Blanc, CF=Cabernet Franc, SY=Syrah, PS=Petite Sirah, JR=Johannisberg Riesling, SH=Shiraz.

Varieties: Z,SG, Pinot Grigio, PN, Arnies, Nebbiolo, Barbera & Port
www.seghesio.com

Silver Oak Cellars
24625 Chianti Road, Geyserville
P.O. Box 558, Geyserville, CA 95441
(707) 857-3562
Open 9-4 Mon-Sat
Closed Holidays & Sundays
Tours by appt at 1:30 • No Sat tours
Cabernet Sauvignon / tasting fee $10 per person, you keep the glass
www.silveroak.com

Simi Winery
16275 Healdsburg Ave., Healdsburg
P.O. Box 698, Healdsburg, CA 95448
(707) 433-6981 or (800) 746-4880
Open 10-5 daily
Seasonal tours & tasting
Dec-Feb 11am & 2pm
Mar-Nov 11am, 1pm & 3pm
(707) 433-6253
Picnic area
Varieties: SB,C,Z,CS,SY,M,PN
www.simiwinery.com

Sommer Vineyards & Winery
5110 Hwy 128
Geyserville, CA 95441
(800) 433-1944
Tours & Tasting by appointment only
Varieties: CS,Z,M, Sangiovese, Port
Currently closed for renovation. Tours by appointment only.
www.sommervineyards.com

Stonestreet
4611 Thomas Road (off Chalk Hill Rd.)
Healdsburg, CA 95448
(707) 433-9463
Tours & Tasting by appointment only
Legacy Varieties: Red Meritage, CS, M, Cabernet Franc Blend
Stonestreet Varieties: CS,M,C,SB,PN
www.legacywine.com
www.stonestreetwines.com

Trentadue Winery
19170 Geyserville Ave., Geyserville
(707) 433-3104
Open 11-4:30 daily
& 320 Center St., Healdsburg
(707) 433-1082 or (888) 332-3032
Open 10-5 daily
Weddings • Special events
Picnic area
Varieties: C,M,CS,SG,PS,Z, Rosé, Port
www.trentadue.com

Wattle Creek
25510 River Road, Cloverdale
Varieties: SH,CS,C,SB
(707) 894-5166; by appointment

White Oak Winery
7505 Hwy 128, Healdsburg, CA 95448
(707) 433-8429
Open 10-5 daily
Picnic grounds • Private parties
Varieties: SB,C,M, "Old Vine" Zin, Myers Ltd. Reserve, Bordeaux-style
www.whiteoakwines.com

C=Chardonnay, CS=Cabernet Sauvignon, M=Merlot, Z=Zinfandel, PN=Pinot Noir, SB=Sauvignon Blanc, V=Viognier, SG=Sangiovese, G=Gewürztraminer, ME=Meritage, FB=Fumé Blanc, CF=Cabernet Franc, SY=Syrah, PS=Petite Sirah, JR=Johannisberg Riesling, SH=Shiraz.

The Index

Recipe	Page

Recipe	Page

Recipe	Page